The Ghosts of Birds

ALSO BY ELIOT WEINBERGER

AUTHOR

Works on Paper (1986) • *Nineteen Ways of Looking at Wang Wei* (1987)
Outside Stories (1992) • *Written Reaction* (1996) • *Karmic Traces* (2000)
9/12 (2003) • *What I Heard About Iraq* (2005)
What Happened Here: Bush Chronicles (2005) • *The Stars* (2005)
Muhammad (2006) • *An Elemental Thing* (2007)
Oranges & Peanuts for Sale (2009) • *Wildlife* (2011)
Two American Scenes (with Lydia Davis, 2013)
The Wall, the City, and the World (2014)

EDITOR & TRANSLATOR

Octavio Paz: *Eagle or Sun?* (1970; 1976) • *A Draft of Shadows* (1980)
Selected Poems (1984) • *Collected Poems 1957–1987* (1987)
A Tree Within (1988) • *Sunstone* (1991) • *In Light of India* (1997)
A Tale of Two Gardens (1997) • *An Erotic Beyond: Sade* (1998)
Figures & Figurations (2002) • *The Poems of Octavio Paz* (2012)
Homero Aridjis: *Exaltation of Light* (1981)
Jorge Luis Borges: *Seven Nights* (1984) • *Selected Non-Fictions* (1999)
Vicente Huidobro: *Altazor* (1988; 2003)
Cecilia Vicuña: *Unravelling Words and the Weaving of Water* (1992)
Xavier Villaurrutia: *Nostalgia for Death* (1992)
Bei Dao: *Unlock* (with Iona Man Cheong, 2000)
The Rose of Time: Selected Poems (2010)

EDITOR

Montemora (1975–1982)
Una antología de la poesía norteamericana desde 1950 (1992)
American Poetry Since 1950: Innovators & Outsiders (1993)
Sulfur 33: Into the Past (1993)
The New Directions Anthology of Classical Chinese Poetry (2003)
World Beat: International Poetry Now from New Directions (2006)
Elsewhere (2014) • *Calligrams: Writings from and on China* (2015–)

Eliot Weinberger

The Ghosts of Birds

A NEW DIRECTIONS PAPERBOOK ORIGINAL

First published as a New Directions Paperbook Original (NDP1355) in 2016.
Manufactured in the United States of America
Design by Erik Rieselbach

Library of Congress Cataloging-in-Publication Data
Names: Weinberger, Eliot, author.
Title: The ghosts of birds / Eliot Weinberger.
Description: First edition. | New York : New Directions Publishing, 2016. |
Includes bibliographical references.
Identifiers: LCCN 2016021273 | ISBN 9780811226189 (softcover : acid-free paper)
Classification: LCC PS3573.E3928 A6 2016 | DDC 814/.54—dc23
LC record available at https://lccn.loc.gov/2016021273

8 9

New Directions Books are published for James Laughlin
by New Directions Publishing Corporation
80 Eighth Avenue, New York 10011

for N. S., A. D. & S.

CONTENTS

II.

The Ghosts of Birds

From a Hymn to the Goddess of the Three Cities

O speck of dust from your lotus feet
O island city of the sun
O waterfall of ghee
O bow made of flowers
O bowstring of bees
O daughter of snow mountain
O coral-tree blossom
O necklace of wishing-jewels
O forest of wishing-trees
O refuge from the world
O lotus of a thousand petals
O full-blown blue lotus
O moon of musk
O liquid drop from a moonstone
O world drinking moonlight
A waterfall of nectar falls from the flowers of the mind

O eyes as shy as a forest deer
O body slender as a lightning bolt
O streak of vermillion in the part of your hair
O curling hair beautiful as young bees
O hair untied and flowing
O forehead like a second half-moon
O eyebrows slightly arched
O eyes like bees
(Day dawns in your right eye
                                        Night falls in your left
and your third eye is the twilight)

3

O feathery eyelashes disrupting tranquility
The world is created when you open your eyes
and dissolves when you close them

O the three creases in your neck
O your four arms soft and slender as the filament of a lotus
O the loveliness of your hands
O your breasts like ruby jars of nectar
O the clothes slipping from your breasts
O the sweating curves of your breasts
O the deep pool of your navel
O the line of abdominal hair like a ripple on a river
O your thighs like golden plantain stalks
O your well-rounded knees
O the soft jangle of your anklets
O the streams of nectar flowing between your feet
O your lotus feet set upon my head

The morning sun opens lotus clusters in the minds of great poets
bright as moonstone slivers   sweet as milk and ghee   sweet
as the lotus fragrance of the mouth of the Queen of Speech
and your earrings slightly jangle as you listen and nod your head
keeping time in wonder and delight   your shining earrings
like little moons reflecting the brightness of your cheeks

You are mind you are space you are the wind and the fire the wind carries
You are the waters and the earth   there is nothing more
This lightless world is flooded with your radiance

4

I.

The Story of Adam and Eve

On June 9, 1603, Samuel de Champlain attended an Algonquin victory ceremony along the banks of the Ottawa River. He sat with the Grand Sagamore, Besouat, in front of a row of spikes topped with the heads of the defeated enemy, and watched as the Grand Sagamore's wives and daughters danced before them entirely naked, wearing only necklaces of dyed porcupine quills.

After the dancing, the conversation turned to theology. The Grand Sagamore told Champlain that there was one sole God. After God had created all things, he stuck some arrows in the ground, and these turned into the men and women who populated the earth.

Champlain told the Grand Sagamore that this was pagan superstition and false. There was indeed one sole God, but after he had created all things, he took a lump of clay and made a man, and then took one of the man's ribs and made a woman. The Grand Sagamore looked doubtful, but following the rules of hospitality, remained silent.

Genesis says surprisingly little about Adam and Eve. In its first account of the creation, God (or the gods: the name is Elohim, which is plural) creates both male and female in his image, declares that they will be the masters of all the beasts on the earth, gives them the seed-bearing plants and the trees with seed-bearing fruit that will be their food—in other words, they are to be vegetarians—and tells them to be fruitful and multiply. There is no Eden, and the couple is unnamed.

The second account, in the following chapter, is the more familiar version. God (now called Yahweh) makes a human (*adam*)—later simply called Adam—out of the dust of soil (*adamah*) and places him in the Garden of Eden to till the land and care for the trees. He is forbidden to eat the fruit of the Tree of the Knowledge of Good and Evil, which will somehow cause his death. Yahweh says nothing about not eating the fruit of the Tree of Life, which would have given Adam immortality.

Yahweh creates Eve out of Adam's rib, though the passage can also be read that she is cleaved from his "side"—possibly meaning that Adam, like the First Person of many mythologies—and Adam himself among the Gnostics—was originally androgynous, and then split in half to form man and woman. They are naked but unashamed.

The serpent—the "shrewdest" or "most subtle" of the beasts—convinces Eve to eat the (unidentified) fruit of the Tree of the Knowledge of Good and Evil, and she gives some to Adam. They now realize they are naked and cover themselves with fig leaves. They hear the sound of Yahweh, who is out having a stroll in the Garden in the cool of the day—a god seemingly made in the image of man—and hide themselves. Yahweh, although omniscient, calls out: Where are you? Adam replies that he's hiding because he's naked and afraid to show himself. Yahweh, though he knows the answer, asks: Who told you were naked? Did you eat the fruit of that tree?

Yahweh condemns Adam to the hard labor of tilling a land full of brambles and thistles, Eve to the hard labor of childbirth, and the serpent to crawling on the ground. Compassionately, he makes clothes for the humans out of skins, presumably slaughtering some of the animals of paradise. (After creating the universe, God then works as a butcher, a tanner, and a tailor.) But with their knowledge of good and evil, the humans have become too much like Yahweh himself. Worried—if God worries—that they will eat the fruit of the Tree of Life and become immortal like him, Yahweh expels them from the Garden, and places a Mesopotamian winged sphinx at the gate with a sword of fire to prevent them from returning.

In the next sentence, Adam and Eve, with their new knowledge, "know" each other, and Cain is born. Eve remarks, mischievously: I have created a man, just like Yahweh. In the sentence after that, she gives birth to Abel. Cain becomes a farmer and Abel a shepherd. Cain makes a sacrifice to Yahweh of some vegetables and Abel of some fatty meat. Yahweh, not a vegetarian when it comes to the smoke of burnt offerings, prefers Abel's sacrifice. Cain is jealous and slays Abel. (This is the first time where the word "sin" appears. Naturally, an institution such as the Church would later consider disobedience and not murder as the Original Sin.) Once again, pretending not to know the answer, Yahweh asks Cain where Abel is. "Am I my brother's keeper?" Yahweh curses Cain and condemns him to a life of exile. Cain complains that the punishment is too great and whoever sees him will kill him. So Yahweh creates an unspecified mark on Cain, which is not a sign of Cain's evil, but a warning to others that he must be left alone. Who the others are, whom he's afraid of, who must leave him alone, is unexplained. Cain is exiled to the Land of Nod ("Wandering"), east of Eden, and, in the next sentence, has sex with an equally inexplicable unnamed wife, who gives birth to Enoch, which sets off a long genealogy.

Genesis was probably written in the 5th century BCE, about the same time that the Buddha was preaching, east of Eden. There is no further information about Adam and Eve for another five hundred years. In the 1st century CE, *The Life of Adam and Eve* may or may not have been written in Hebrew or an undetermined Semitic language. It survives in Greek, Latin, Slavonic, Georgian, and Armenian versions, and was translated or adapted scores of times throughout the Middle Ages. (The Greek version is also known as *The Apocalypse of Moses*, for it claims to be the story that God told to Moses after he descended the mountain with the Tablets of the Law.) Adam lays dying at age 930, and the account of the expulsion is told, unusually, in flashbacks—briefly by Adam and later at length by Eve to her thirty sons and daughters gathered around her. They don't understand what is happening, because Adam is the first person to die of old age. The book ends with long descriptions of the deaths and burials of both.

A major theme is food and hunger, and the Armenian, Georgian, and Latin versions even open with Adam and Eve starving. Perhaps this is the key to the book's universality: The predominant human condition after the Fall is not the shame of sin but hunger.

It is not the serpent who tempts Eve, but Satan who tempts the serpent, asking him why he's eating weeds, while Adam and Eve are enjoying the fruits of paradise, and suggesting that he can cast the humans out and eat all the fruit himself. Satan then speaks through the mouth of the serpent, who appears to Eve as an angel. (Eve is naive, not wicked.) As soon as she eats the fruit, the leaves on all the trees except the fig wither; the Garden becomes the Waste Land. She uses the surviving fig leaves to cover herself.

Expelled from paradise, they are hungry. In the Armenian version: "They sought and they did not find vegetable sustenance like that which was in the Garden," because, as Eve later explains, "God established this vegetable food as food for the beasts that they might eat on the earth, but our food is that which the angels eat." In the Georgian version, Eve suggests they kill an animal to eat, but Adam is appalled. In the Slavonic version, Adam considers letting Eve starve to death, but then realizes that she too is God's creation, which he has no right to destroy. In the Latin version, Eve asks Adam to kill her, so that he may return to paradise. He responds: "Don't say such things, Eve, lest the Lord God bring upon us some other curse. How could it be that I should raise my hand against my own flesh?"

They hope that if they perform a penance God will help, and they stand in rivers up to their necks, with heavy stones on their feet: Adam in the Jordan for forty days and Eve in the Tigris for thirty-four days (because she is six days younger). In most of the versions they stand in silence with their hair floating on the water, but in the Georgian: "Adam raised his voice towards God and he varied his tone of voice six times, like the voices of all the angels in all times." Eve is tempted again by Satan and comes out of the river, water-logged, her beauty gone, looking like "withered grass" or "rotten vegetables." God ultimately gives them food, and teaches them to sow and reap.

In the Armenian version, Eve, full of shame that she has again fallen to temptation, goes off to live by herself. She gives birth to Cain in a hut, attended by an angel. Cain's body is the "color of stars"— perhaps this implies unnatural paleness. As soon as he is born, Cain leaps up and begins to pull out the grass around the hut, "and infertilities became numerous in that place."

In the Georgian version of the Cain and Abel story, two demons take their forms, and demon Cain slays demon Abel with a transparent stone sword. The human Cain watches this, and is inspired. In the Greek version, Adam and Eve know that Abel has been murdered because Eve dreams that the blood of Abel is being poured into Cain's mouth, which he gulps down and vomits. In the Slavonic version, after Abel is killed, God strangely tells the archangel Michael: "Warn Adam: 'You should not say anything to your son Cain about this matter, and don't be troubled on account of it, instead keep it in your hearts.'"

The death of Adam is an elaborate spectacle in the sky, with gold censers and chariots of fire and angels and cherubims and seraphs weeping and imploring God to forgive Adam. In the Georgian version, Eve has a bizarre confusion. She mistakes the sun and the moon, who are also prostrate and beseeching the Lord, for Indians.

The Latin version is more Christianized than the others. Adam is created in the place that will become Bethlehem, where Jesus will be born, and then taken to the Garden. (And in later stories, the seed planted on Adam's grave will become the tree from which the wood of the Cross is made.) Adam is made not only in the image of God, but as a microcosm of the universe. Four angels are sent in the four directions over the earth to gather the dust that will form him, mixed with the waters of the four rivers that flow from paradise (the Tigris, the Euphrates, the unidentified Pishon, and the Gihon, which may or may not be the Nile). On their journeys, each angel sees the ruling star of that quadrant: Ancolim in the east, Disis in the south, Arthos in the north, and Mencembrion in the west. The sky creates his name.

Moreover, human frailty is attributable not to human nature, but to nature itself, embedded in our cells:

> It must be known that the body of Adam was formed of eight parts. The first part was of the dust of the earth, from which was made his flesh, and thereby he was sluggish. The next part was of the sea, from which was made his blood, and thereby he was aimless and fleeing. The third part was of the stones of the earth, from which his bones were made, and thereby he was hard and covetous. The fourth part was of the clouds, from which were made his thoughts, and thereby he was immoderate. The fifth part was of the wind, from which was made his breath, and thereby he was fickle. The sixth part was of the sun, from which were made his eyes, and thereby he was handsome and beautiful. The seventh part was of the light of the world, from which he was made pleasing, and thereby he had knowledge. The eighth part was of the Holy Spirit, from which was made his soul, and thereby are the bishops, priests, and all the saints and elect of God.

The Latin version also explains that we know the story of Adam and Eve because the dying Eve had instructed her son Seth to write it down. The archangel Michael has told her that the world will be destroyed by water or by fire, so she tells Seth to write it on two stelae, one of stone and one of clay, for if God "judges our race by water, the tablets of earth will dissolve, but the tablets of stone will endure. If, however, he judges our race by fire, the tablets of stone will be destroyed, but the tablets of earth will be fired." An angel guides Seth's hand as he writes, and what he writes is called *achiliacae*, defined in the text itself as "writing without the teaching of words." Generations see the stelae, but no one can read them until long after the Flood, when an angel appears to Solomon and gives him the knowledge of this indecipherable language.

The most comprehensive history, *The Book of Adam and Eve* (also known as *The Conflict of Adam and Eve with Satan*) was translated from a lost Arabic original into Ge'ez (Ethiopic) in the 5th or 6th century. It is also the basis for—or derives from the same source as—*The Book of the Cave of Treasures*, which is traditionally attributed to Ephrem the Syrian, a known historical figure, although he predates his own book by two centuries.

Adam and Eve opens with the expulsion. Along with the realization of their nakedness, the humans discover that they are walking ("They trod the ground on their feet, not knowing they were treading"). They see the world stretched out before them, covered with rocks and sand, and faint. God sends them to the Mountain of Eden to live in a cave, which they find claustrophobic and gloomy. They pray "in their own language, unknown to us." (That would be the language in which Adam named all the animals in Genesis, so their true names remain equally lost. Adam would later tell Dante in heaven that his language became extinct before the time of Nimrod, but others say it was the universal language spoken by the builders of the Tower of Babel.) Adam gazes up toward the heavens, but sees only the overhanging rock, and faints again.

In paradise they had extraordinary vision, called "bright nature," but now they are nearsighted. They leave the cave and come upon the unidentified body of water that flows to the roots of the Tree of Life and then splits into the four rivers. They try to drown themselves. An angel rescues them and believes they are dead. God brings them back to life, and tells them they must now drink water to live and must wash themselves—apparently in paradise they did neither. Adam asks to return to the Garden; God, for the moment, stops talking to him. They refuse to drink water, thinking it will harm them.

Night falls and they can't understand why they can no longer see each other; in paradise it was always day, but in some form of indirect light. When dawn rises, Adam comes out of the cave, sees the flaming sun, feels its heat, and thinks he will be burned to death.

On the first morning they encounter the serpent, once the "fairest of all beasts" and now the ugliest, slippery and crawling on the ground. It still speaks and tries to kill Eve. God strikes it dumb and calls up a great wind to blow the serpent away. It lands on the seashore in India.

The day grows hot; they are sweating and exhausted by their new task of walking. Again, like characters in an existentialist novel, they attempt suicide, flinging themselves off a cliff. Again God resuscitates them. Bruised and bloody, they build an altar of stones, wipe their blood off with leaves, gather the bloodstained dust, and offer their blood to God. God is pleased, sends a blazing fire to consume the offering and, frighteningly, smells its "sweet savor." Seeing that he has won God's favor, Adam wants to kill himself as an even greater offering, but God dissuades him.

They return to the cave depressed, so God instructs the angels to cheer them up with their first worldly goods: seventy rods of gold, twelve pounds of incense, and three pounds of myrrh. The gold will give off light at night; the incense will make the cave smell sweet; the myrrh will comfort them. Their home is now known as the Cave of Treasures.

Seven days have passed and they still have neither eaten nor drunk. They stand in the rivers in penitence. Eve is again tempted by Satan. Forty-two days have passed; they are starving and beseech God for food. He instructs a cherub to bring them each one fig from the Garden. The figs are the size of watermelons, for fruit is much larger in paradise, yet they stubbornly refuse to eat them, and ask God for the fruit from the Tree of Life and water from the Water of Life. This, of course, is impossible.

Fifty days have passed. They have been tempted over and over by Satan, and they are cold and naked. God tells them to go to the seashore where they will find the skins of animals that have been eaten by lions, and he sends an angel to teach them how to sew clothes. Meanwhile, the figs have been stolen by Satan and buried. God makes them grow into giant trees full of fruit, in whose shade the humans may rest, but then capriciously changes the trees back into two large figs, which he orders Adam and Eve to eat. Moreover, he has "put into them a mixture as of savory bread and blood"—no doubt, in this Christian text, so that humans will develop a taste for Communion. On the eighty-third day, they finally eat, but become ill because they have no digestive organs. God remedies that, but Adam and Eve, "now that their bodies had strange functions," realize they can never return to paradise. "Henceforth we are earthy." But they get their first good night's sleep from all the food they've eaten.

Adam goes to work the next morning, and God shows him how to grow wheat and bake bread. Satan tempts or attacks the couple fourteen times: burning their cave, throwing boulders at them, stabbing Adam, appearing as a lion, as an angel, as a kindly old man, as a group of beautiful maidens bathing. The latter puts ideas in Adam's head, but he waits for God to consecrate his marriage to Eve on the two hundred and twenty-third day. He gives her the gold rods as a wedding gift.

Eve gives birth to Cain and his twin sister, Luluwa, who is more beautiful than her mother. After they are weaned, Eve has another set of twins: Abel and Aklia, who is "ill-favored." Cain is hard-hearted, sullen, and angry; Abel meek, pious, and obedient. They are not a happy family: Eve dislikes Cain; God "abhors" him. Cain even beats Eve, but she refuses to tell Adam. The parents intend Abel to marry the beautiful Luluwa and Cain the less-beautiful Aklia. God is pleased with Abel's offerings and rejects the offerings from Cain. Cain clubs Abel, then smashes his head with a stone. The earth trembles receiving

Abel's blood, and the Mark of Cain is that he will permanently tremble.

Cain marries Luluwa, without their parent's consent, and implicitly without hers. They go off and have many children, and nothing more is heard of Luluwa. Seven years later, Eve gives birth to Seth, who is more handsome than his father. When he turns fifteen, they marry him to Aklia, who is thirty-seven. Seth does not want to marry, but is obedient to his parents.

Hundreds of years pass. The dying Adam tells Seth that his descendants must not mix with the descendants of Cain. The descendants of Seth live in a state of ecstasy on the Holy Mountain: they do no work, but spend all their time in prayer, living off the fruit of trees. They are the "most happy and just tribe of people who has ever lived." Cain has innumerable descendants, for they are "given to animal lusts." They are thieves and sinners, and in the end Cain is murdered by his grandson, Lamech the Blind.

Lamech the Blind has a son, Genun, who becomes the leader of the Tribe of Cain. He invents musical instruments—"sundry trumpets and horns, and string instruments, cymbals, and psalteries, and lyres and harps, and flutes," and plays "at all times and at every hour . . . beautiful and sweet sounds that ravished the heart." He invents corn liquor and establishes "drink-houses" for the men. Satan teaches him about iron and how to make weapons of war, with which the men kill each other, and how to make flashy clothes by dyeing them purple and crimson. The pious and ascetic sons of Seth are lured down from their mountain. They are smitten by the beautiful tattooed faces of the daughters of Cain; the daughters of Cain fall on the handsome sons of Seth "like ravenous beasts" and the world is abominable until the Flood.

The children of the sons of Seth and the daughters of Cain may or not be the Nephilim, the mysterious giants who roam the land in Genesis. Or the Nephilim may be the sons of Seth themselves, or fallen

16

angels, or the children of fallen angels and human women. There are many theories. In 1705, Cotton Mather discovered some mastodon bones and teeth near Albany, New York, and declared they were the remains of Nephilim who had died in the Flood.

Genesis and all the other books are silent on the nature of the serpent, before it was cursed by God and turned into a snake. Hundreds of years later, an Ethiopian monk finally explained that the serpent was an animal called a "taman." It looked like a baby camel.

Everyone agrees that in paradise it was eternally spring; the seasons and the geographical extremes of climate began after the Fall. Augustine in the 5th century, and Arnold of Bonneval and Honoré d'Autun in the 12th wrote that, in Eden, Adam never had an erection. Had their been no Fall, Augustine said, "speaking of things . . . so far as possible as they could have been before they were matters to be ashamed of," "it was possible for the man's seed to enter into his wife's womb with the integrity of the female organ unbroken." Honoré believed that their children would have spoken and walked at birth. Alexander Neckam in the 13th century noted that there were no flies, gnats, fleas, or other pests in paradise, and Eve did not menstruate there. In the 12th century, Hildegard of Bingen said that in Eden Adam could sing like an angel and "knew every kind of music," but after the fall he was overcome with melancholy and carnal pleasures, and his voice changed to typical male jeering and boorish laughter.

In 1655, Isaac La Peyrère solved the problems of all the people in Genesis outside of Adam's immediate family and all the subsequent races of humankind by declaring that God had created other people before Adam, that Adam was only the first Jew, and that, since the Old Testament was confined to the story of the Jews, the Flood had merely covered the Holy Land and left the rest of the world and its peoples intact.

In 1691, an English magazine was asked the question: Who was Cain afraid would kill him? The answer was: the people of the future.

Most of the sources say that Adam and Eve spent a total of three hours in paradise, though some say six. In the Hebrew apocryphal book Jubilees, all the birds and animals—"whatever walked or moved"—were expelled from the Garden along with the humans. Only plant life remained.

The World

[2nd century BCE]

To the north are the People Who Walk on Tiptoes, the Deep-Eyed
    People, the People Without Anuses, and the One-Eyed People.
To the south are the People With Bound Breasts, the Winged Peo-
    ple, the Naked People, the Cross-Legged People, the Pierced-
    Breast People, the People Who Never Die, the Tongue-Tied
    People, the Hog-Snouted People, the Chisel-Toothed People,
    the Three-Headed People, and the People With Long Arms.
To the west are the Sky People, the White People, the Male People,
    the Female People, the People With Long Thighs, the People
    With One Leg, the People With One Arm, and the People With
    Three Bodies.
To the east are the Black-Toothed People, the Dark-Legged People,
    the Hairy People, and the Hardworking People.

The people in the north are as stupid as animals but live long.
The people in the south mature early but die young.
The people in the west are daring but not humane. The men have
    unfortunate faces and misshapen necks, but they walk with
    dignity.
The people in the east are tall and large. They become knowledge-
    able early but do not live long.
The people in the center are clever and sagelike. We consider
    beards beautiful and dislike obesity.

There is a mountain called Hanging Gardens.
If you manage to climb it, you will be able to control the wind and
    the rain.

19

There is a mountain called Cool Wind.
If you manage to climb it, you will never die.

The Great Meadow, known as the Impenetrable;
the Misty Meadow;
the Endless Meadow, known as the Great Dream;
the Island of Wealth;
the Meadow of Springs, known as the Nine Districts;
the Ocean of Meadow, known as Bactria;
the Frozen Meadow, known as the Great Obscurity.

The Harmonious Hill, known as the Wasteland;
the Forest of Thorns;
the Horde of Women, known as the Great Destitution;
the Backwards-Facing Doors;
the Fiery Earth, known as Scorched Pygmies;
the Fertile Wilderness, known as Metal Hill;
the Place of Sands, called One Eye;
the Gathering Ice, called Abandoned Wings.

In the northeast is the Land of Beginning Again.
In the east is the Land of Seclusion.

Islands in the Sea

In Ireland in the 8th century, there was a man of war named Ailill of the Edge of Battle, from the tribe of the Eoganacht of Ninuss. He went with his king on a raid to another district. They camped near a convent. At midnight, when the camp was asleep, Ailill went to the convent. He saw a young nun come out to strike the bell for nocturne. He grabbed her by the hand.

The men ravaged and took hostages and returned to Ninuss. Soon after, marauders from Leix trapped Ailill in the church of Dubcluain and burned it down. The nun gave birth to a son, whom she named Mael Duin, and gave him secretly to the queen of her tribe.

Mael Duin thought he was the son of the king and queen and that his three foster brothers were his brothers. He came to know his true origins, and went with his brothers to Ninuss, where he was welcomed. Standing in the charred ruins of the church of Dubcluain, he learned how his father had been killed by the marauders from Leix. He swore to take revenge. He was told that the only way to Leix was by sea.

He went to the country of Corcomroe to seek a charm and the blessing of the druid Nuca there. The druid told him the day he should begin building his boat, and the day he should set out. He told him that he must have seventeen men with him, no more or less.

Mael Duin built his three-skin boat and gathered his seventeen men. On the appointed day, they set sail. But his three brothers insisted they must go, and swam far out following the boat. Fearing they would drown, Mael Duin took them on board.

That night they came to two small and bare islands with forts on them. Inside they could hear the drunken soldiers. One of them was loudly bragging how he had slain Ailill of the Edge of Battle and no kinsman had come to avenge the death. Mael Duin and the men prepared to attack.

A great wind suddenly arose and they were driven out to sea, with no sight of land. Mael Duin blamed his brothers for disobeying the word of the druid, and the brothers were silent. Mael Duin declared that no one should row, that the boat should drift wherever God wanted it to go.

Three days and nights they drifted, and then heard the sound of waves breaking on a shore. As they were about to land, a swarm of ants, each the size of a colt, came down the beach toward them, and swam out after them as the men furiously rowed away.

They rowed and came to an island that was all terraced, with trees growing on every level, and countless birds in the trees. No one was there. They caught, and cooked, and ravenously ate the birds.

They came to a large and flat island, and found an enormous mowed lawn with the hoof-prints of horses on it. Each hoof-print was the length of a ship's mast. Scattered on the green were the shells of huge nuts and piles of plunder. The men fled, and when they were out to sea again, they heard the sound of a horse race and the roar of a vast crowd cheering.

A week of rowing, in hunger and thirst. They came to an island with a great house facing the sea. Inside they found a canopied bed for the head of the house, and a bed for every three members of the household. Food was piled before every bed, and a glass vessel with a liquor, and glass cups beside every vessel. No one was there. They ate and drank and slept.

They came to an island that seemed delightful, with many animals like horses. But the animals were tearing pieces out of each other's sides with their teeth, and carrying off the skin and flesh. Blood streamed from their sides; the ground was covered with it. The men fled hastily and grew sad, wondering where they were going in the world.

Hungry and thirsty, sad and sighing, without hope, they came to an island with many trees of golden apples. From sunset to dawn, short red animals like pigs would come out from underground caverns and kick the trees with their hind limbs to make the apples fall. The men landed and found the apples delicious, but the ground was so hot they could not linger on that land.

Long after their store of apples had run out, they came to an island with a great fort of burnt lime, surrounded by white houses, dazzling in the sun. They saw no one, only a small cat, playing on four stone pillars, leaping from one to another. There was a roasted ox and vessels of good liquor, white quilts and shining garments. Pinned to a wall were a row of silver and gold brooches and a row of silver and gold necklaces and a row of swords with hilts of silver and gold. They ate and drank and slept, and the cat played on the pillars. When they decided to move on, Mael Duin's third brother asked if he could take one of the necklaces. Mael Duin said no, for this house has a guard. The brother ignored him and took the treasure. The cat followed him and then leapt like a fiery arrow and burnt him to ashes. Mael Duin soothed the cat with his words, put the necklace back in its place, swept up the ashes and cast them into the sea.

They came to an island with great flocks of sheep divided in two by a bronze wall. On one side the sheep were all black, on the other the sheep were all white. An enormous man was sorting the flocks. He would take a black sheep and throw it over the wall and it would turn white. He would take a white sheep and throw it over the wall and it would turn black. The men were afraid and did not land.

They came to an island with countless pigs. They caught a small one, but despite its size they could not lift it, so they roasted it on the spot. On that island was a wide river. One of the men dipped his sword in, and the sword instantly dissolved.

They came to an island with crowds of people dressed in black and weeping. Mael Duin's second brother drew the lot to scout ahead. He went ashore and fell to weeping with the rest and would not return.

They came to an island with four walls: a wall of gold, a wall of silver, a wall of brass, and a wall of crystal. Kings occupied one quarter, queens another, warriors the third and maidens the fourth. When they landed, a maiden came to greet them and brought them a food like cheese and an intoxicating liquor. The men slept for three days and three nights, and when they awoke they were on their boat again, far out to sea.

They came to an island with a great fortress, entered by a bridge of glass. The men fell backward trying to cross it. A maiden appeared, with golden hair and a gold circlet around her head, sandals of pure silver and a silken smock next to her white skin. She welcomed each of the men by name and said their arrival had long been foreseen. She brought them into the castle, where there was a bed for Mael Duin and a bed for every three of the men. She fed them a food like cheese and an intoxicating liquor. The men asked if she would sleep with Mael Duin, but she refused, and the next morning when they awoke they were on their boat again, far out to sea.

At sea they heard a strange chanting coming across the waters, and rowed toward the sound for a night and a day until they came to an island with a high mountain, full of black birds that were never silent. They found a man there whose clothing was the hair that fell to his ankles, who told them that he was a man of Ireland who had been lost at sea, that angels came to feed him every day, and that the birds

24

were the souls of his children and his kinsmen, who were waiting for the end of time.

The sea became like green glass and they could see clearly the rocks and sand at the bottom of it, and the fish swimming by. Then they saw, beneath the sea, a beautiful village with houses and grazing flocks of cattle. A hideous beast appeared, stretched out its long neck to snatch the largest ox in the herd, and devoured it in a flash. They saw the villagers flee in terror, and they rowed on.

They came to an island with a stream that rose from the shore and crossed over the whole island like a rainbow. They could walk under it without getting wet. Salmon were falling out of the stream, trying to swim across, and the island stank of rotting fish.

They came upon a great column rising out of the sea, with no land around it. From the top of the column, somewhere in the clouds, they could hear a man speaking in a language they did not understand.

They came to an island that was a great plain, with a crowd of people who never stopped laughing. Mael Duin's third brother went to join them, and began to laugh as though he had always lived there, and would not return to the boat.

There was a small island with a wall of fire revolving around it and an open doorway in the wall. Whenever the doorway passed by them, they could see the inhabitants within: handsome men and women with adorned clothes, feasting with gold vessels in their hands. They could hear delightful songs, but the wall of fire was spinning too quickly for them to enter.

They came to an island with abundant cattle, but no houses on it, and ate for days. A falcon landed on the island, and Mael Duin saw that it was like the falcons of Ireland. They watched as the bird flew off to the southeast, and they rowed after it.

In Ireland, gone for so many years and long presumed dead, they were welcomed in astonishment. Mael Duin returned to his kinsmen in Ninuss, though he had never avenged his father's death.

A Journey on the Colorado River
[1869]

The Indians say that once there was a great chief who was inconsolable in his mourning for his wife. The god Ta-vwoats appeared to him, and offered to carve a trail through the mountains and take him to paradise, to show him that his wife was in a happier land. When they returned, the chief was made to promise that he would never reveal where he had been, for his people, living in the harshness of the desert, would all want to follow that trail to paradise. Then, mindful of human frailties, the god Ta-vwoats sent a mad and raging river down that trail: the canyon gorges of the Colorado.

We raise our little flags and push the boats from shore.

I know not, O I know not,
what joys await us there

Curiously shaped buttes. The head of the first canyon: bright vermillion rocks. We name this Flaming Gorge.

With not a little anxiety, we enter the mysterious canyon. They say it can't be run. The Indians say: "Water heap catch 'em."

> *Timorous mortals start and shrink,*
> *and linger shivering on the brink,*
> *and fear to launch away*

The first rapids. We thread the passage with exhilarating velocity, foaming crests above us as we plunge into troughs.

The great relief when we reach the quiet water below. The canyon is in the shape of an elongated U, and we name it Horseshoe Canyon.

Kingfishers play about the streams. We name these places Kingfisher Creek, Kingfisher Park, and Kingfisher Canyon.

Hundreds of swallows flit about the cliffs like swarms of bees; we name it Beehive Point.

> The landscape revels in the sunshine.

> *Awake, my soul, and with the sun*
> *thy daily stage of duty run*

Dangerous rapids, and then more dangerous rapids. An old Indian had told me about this canyon: "The rocks heap heap high, the water go hooo-woogh, hoo-woogh . . . "

> *From many an ancient river,*
> *from many a palmy plain,*

they call us to deliver
their land from error's chain

No rocks in the way: railroad speed. Our boats ride the waves like startled deer leaping over fallen trees.

The daylight is serene

Calm water. A threatening roar in the distance.

High on the rocks above, an inscription:

ASHLEY 18 5.

Is it 1835 or 1855? We had heard tell of a party that had once attempted the river and drowned.

Frail children of dust, and feeble as frail

We name the cataract here Ashley Falls.

The little valleys above are beautiful parks, decked with flowers: blue eyes, painted cups, the fragrant white blossoms of spirea. Mule-deer and elk abound; grizzlies, wolverines, mountain cats. The music of birds; the noisy brooks; the snow fields gleaming in the distance.

29

The whole creation join in one

The barren wilderness shall smile,
with sudden greens and herbage crown'd;
and streams shall murmur all around

The glory of landscape.

Cliffs full of swallows.

Wandering swallows that long to find their wonted rest

Chicks peep out from the doorways of their mud houses.
We name this Swallow Canyon.

Warblers, woodpeckers, flickers above; meadow larks in the grass;
wild geese in the river.

Swift as an eagle cuts the air

A lark my Jenny Lind.

Sun going down; shadows creep over the canyon: portal to the region
of gloom we are to enter tomorrow. Only a crescent of night sky and a

single star can be seen above us. We build a campfire of driftwood and the men tell stories of the battlefields of the South. I cannot sleep.

> *Though in paths of death I tread,*
> *with gloomy horrors overhead,*
> *my steadfast heart shall fear no ill*

The river is:
"Recoiling, turmoiling and toiling and boiling,
And gleaming and streaming and steaming and beaming,
And rushing and flushing and brushing and gushing,
And flapping and rapping and clapping and slapping,
And curling and whirling and purling and twirling,
And thumping and plumping and bumping and jumping,
And dashing and flashing and splashing and clashing;
And so never ending, but always descending,
Sounds and motions for ever and ever are blending,
All at once and all o'er, with a mighty uproar,"
So we name this canyon the Canyon of Lodore.

Barely escape, lose one of our boats and its cargo of provisions, though all the men are safely ashore. There, on a small sand beach, covered with driftwood, we find an iron bake oven, some tin plates, a piece of a hull and other fragments. This is where Ashley's party perished.

> *Time, like an ever-rolling stream, bears all its sons away;*
> *they fly, forgotten, as a dream dies at the opening day*

Tired, bruised, and glad to sleep.

Dark and cheerless is the morn

We name this Disaster Falls.

Everything wet and spoiling.

Chase our gloom away

Three cataracts in succession; we name them Triplet Falls, and this stretch of river beset with boulders Hell's Half-Mile.

It seems a long way up to the world of sunshine.

Camped in a grove of cedars, box-elder, and dead willows. A sudden whirlwind scatters our fire and sets the site ablaze. We rush for the boats, ears scorched, hair and clothes singed, carrying what we can. The cook stumbles and falls, and away goes the mess-kit down the river. Plates are gone; spoons gone; our knives and forks are gone.

The unceasing roar of rushing water.

Stopping to make astronomic observations for latitude and longitude: *sweet day of rest!*

Twelve repetitions of a single shout: we name these cliffs
Echo Park.

While fields and floods,
rocks, hills, and plains
repeat the sounding joy

The waters waltz their way through the canyon and our boats spin wildly in whirlpools past the projecting rocks.

We do not know where we are going.

While I am a pilgrim here
let Thy love my spirit cheer

In the evening, camped at the mouth of a small creek, a good supper of trout as we discuss whether to name this place Whirlpool Canyon or Craggy Canyon. We cannot decide.

A headlong ride, rearing and plunging with the waves. We decide to call it Whirlpool Canyon.

Repairing the boats, which have had hard knocks, collecting fossils. Hawkins goes off to hunt and returns with a fine, fat deer. We name the mountain after him: Mount Hawkins.

> The waters troubled with billows, white with foam. Mad
> waves roar.

Split Mountain Canyon. Two or three rapids, then a run of six or eight. Swallows clamor at our intrusion, but the waters drown out their squawking.

> Three falls in close succession.

> *'Tis a strait and thorny road,*
> *and mortal spirits tire and faint*

Sheering around the rocks, heading into a long chute, expecting to be dashed at any second.

Gently flowing past groves and natural meadows. Herds of antelopes feeding, and now and then a wolf. The Indians call this *Won-sits Yu-av*, Antelope Valley.

> *It breathes in the air, it shines in the light,*
> *it streams from the hills, it descends to the plain,*
> *and sweetly distills in the dew and the rain*

Canyon walls rising almost imperceptibly.

We sweep around curve
after curve.

And still new beauties may I see,
and still increasing light

The wind annoys us much today. Piles of broken rocks, a long line of broken cliffs, stunted cedars—ugly clumps, like war clubs with spines. A region of the wildest desolation; we name it the Canyon of Desolation.

Guide me through the dreadful shade

Break an oar in a rapid, then lose another. Two oars left, not enough to pull us through. The river makes a sharp turn and a reflex wave rolls the boat over. Our blankets, two guns, and a barometer are thrown out and gone. Hereafter we may sleep cold.

Though in a bare and rugged way,
through devious, lonely wilds I stray

Bad rapids. Bradley is knocked over the side; his foot catches under the seat and he is dragged, head under water. Camped on a sand beach, the wind blows a hurricane. Sand piles over us like a snowdrift.

Sand plains, naked and drifting, extend on either side as far as the eye can see, glaring in the midday July sun. The reflected heat produces a curious motion in the atmosphere: currents trembling and moving in many directions. It gives the impression of an unstable land.

Strange black bluffs. We stop for an hour or two, take a short walk up the valley. Arrowheads scattered about; flint chips in great profusion; the trails well worn.

The water is quiet, but the course tortuous.

At this bend of the river, the canyons look like three alcoves; we name it Trin-Alcove Bend. We climb the rocks and see the Azure Cliffs, and beyond them the Brown Cliffs, and beyond mountain peaks piled with clouds.

While I am a pilgrim here

Six miles down the river and we're a quarter-mile from where we started. Another nine miles and we're six hundred yards from where the bend began. The men call it a bow-knot of river, so we name it Bow-Knot Bend.

A charge to keep I have, a charge to keep I have

There is an exquisite charm in our ride today. In fine spirits, we whistle, shout, discharge pistols to hear the reverberations from the cliffs. We name this Labyrinth Canyon.

> We pass tower cliffs and name this stretch of
> the river Tower Park.

Region of naked rock, a smooth undulating pavement of beautiful red sandstone. The Indians call this *Toom-pin Tu-weap*, Rock Land. To the south a butte in the form of a fallen cross that we name the Butte of the Cross.

> *While in this darksome wild I stray,*
> *be Thou my light, be Thou my way*

A weird, grand region: everything is rock. Cliffs of rock, tables of rock, plateaus of rock, terraces of rock, crags of rock. No plants, no soil, no sand.

Not piles of boulders or heaps of fragments. A land of bare rock. Buttes as big as cathedrals, cliffs that cannot be scaled, hollow domes, amphitheaters, tall pinnacles that shrink the river to insignificance. Never lichened, never covered with moss.

> *Ah this nor pen nor tongue can show*

Bonita Bend. The Orange Cliffs. Stillwater Canyon.

These streams unite in solemn depths.

My soul with heavenly thoughts supply

Spoiled bacon and bread made from musty flour. Naturally we spend our dinner speaking of better fare.

Wherever we look there is but a wilderness of rocks. The day is spent walking through strange scenes: rock forms that we do not understand.

O'er the gloomy hills of darkness, look, my soul! be still—and gaze

Curious how a little obstacle becomes a great obstruction.

Bad rapids in succession; three oars lost. Camped on the left bank with barely room to lie down.

Boats leaking again.

Difficult rapids and falls, more abrupt than any. We name this Cataract Canyon.

And then the river is broad and swift, through a gorge, grand beyond description. Vertical cliffs reflected in the quiet water; we seem to be in the depths of the earth.

> *Death, like a narrow sea,*
> *divides this heavenly land from ours*

How will it be in the future?

Great angular blocks have fallen from the walls. Among them, the water finds its way, tumbling down in chutes, whirlpools, and great waves, with rushing breakers and foam. I sit on a rock and listen to the roar.

> *From every stormy wind that blows,*
> *from every swelling tide of woes,*
> *there is a calm, a sure retreat*

Caught in a whirlpool and set spinning about.

The canyon is narrower than any we've seen: the water fills from cliff to cliff with no place to land in case of danger. The walls overhead almost shut out the light. I stand on the deck, watching with intense anxiety.

39

Oh could we make our doubts remove,
those gloomy doubts that rise

But it turns out there are no obstructions or
rocks or falls.

The clouds ye so much dread are big with mercy,
and shall break its blessings on your head

The fear of what might have been ahead has made a deep impression
on us. We name it Narrow Canyon.

A cool, pleasant ride round gentle curves. Royal arches, mossy alcoves, deep glens, grottoes seemingly painted.

The ruins of a three-story house, its wall of stone laid in mortar with
much regularity. Flint chips, arrowheads, and pottery shards in great
profusion around. Hundreds of etchings on the cliff face.

Curious mounds and cones, deep holes full of water. In one of them,
twenty feet deep, a tree is growing—the hole so narrow I can step
from the edge to a limb, and climb down this growing ladder.

There ever-lasting spring abides
and never-withering flowers

A vast chamber carved out of the rock, a little grove of box-elder and cottonwoods at the entrance; a deep, clear pool of water, bordered with verdure at one end. A thousand feet above, a narrow, winding skylight. The rock at the ceiling is hard, the rock below soft and friable—thus the great chamber was excavated by a little stream that only runs when the rain falls, so rarely, in this arid country.

We camp in the chamber. The rock is full of sounds as though it were an academy of music designed by an unknown architect and built by storms. We name it Music Temple.

We keep our camp, sleep another night in Music Temple.

> *softly now the light of day*
> *fades upon my sight away*

> *fast falls the eventide, the darkness deepens*

> *Great Guardian of my sleeping hours*
> *thou spread'st the curtains of the night*

> *from many an ancient river,*
> *they call us*

> *oh where shall rest be found*

watchman, tell us of the night,
what its signs of promise are

bright morning star bids darkness flee

shine through the gloom

point me to the skies!

Hsiao Kuan

In the 11th century, Hsiao Kuan dreamed that he was taken to a palace where the women were goddesses or transcendents. All were dressed in green. One of them gave him a piece of paper and said: "This is ripple paper. Would you please write a poem about a winter morning?"
  He wrote:

The twelve towers of the palace hide women dressed in green.
Wine flows from lion-spouts, spiced and fragrant,
trickling through tubes called "thirsty crows."
A servant turns the pulley, red liquid jade spurts out.
Incense barely smoking, lotus candles almost gone,
the five dragons of the clepsydra overflow with chilly water.
Unaccompanied ladies, fish pendants dangling from crimson
    sashes,
stand on tiptoe to watch the sun come up, far off in Fu-sang.
A half-disk lifts above the ripples and the reddening duckweed in
    the lake.
The women turn, look back over the rooftops at the colors of
    clouds.
Courtiers with swords clanging descend from the sky.
Tall hats and armor fill the pavilion hall.

  The transcendent read it and said: "Your poem certainly contains many unusual phrases."

Hsieh Ling-yün

Hsieh Ling-yün, in the 12th century, used to write poems together with his cousin, Hsieh Hui-lien. One day, his cousin was away, and Hsieh Ling-yün had trouble composing. That night, his cousin appeared in a dream, and together they wrote:

> Spring grass grows beside the pond,
> the garden is full of singing birds.

Hsieh Ling-yün believed that he had written these lines thanks to divine intervention.

44

Agate

The *Tso Chuan*, a Chinese history from approximately the 3rd century BCE, records that an official of Lu dreamed that he was crossing the Huan River. Someone gave him pieces of agate as food. He wept, and his tears turned to pieces of agate that filled his arms. He sang a song:

> I crossed the Huan River,
> and was given pieces of agate.
> Go back! Go back!
> My arms are full
> with pieces of agate.

When he awoke, he was afraid and dared not ask to have the dream interpreted, for he knew that pieces of agate are placed in the mouths of the dead.

The years passed, and his power grew. Confident that the pieces of agate symbolized his great number of followers, he arrogantly asked for the dream to be interpreted. The true meaning of the dream was told, and he died that night.

Surviving Fragments from Lost Zoroastrian Books

*

There where the sun rises

*

The edge of a razor

*

Of knowledge, not love

*

The several kinds of wheat

*

All good thoughts I think willingly; all good words I say willingly; all good deeds I do willingly. All evil thoughts I think unwillingly; all evil words I say unwillingly; all evil deeds I do unwillingly.

*

The skin on the head
[...]
The head of a man
[...]
One bone of the skull
[...]
All the blows that [...] the skull are counted

*

One whose words are accepted

*

As much as the earth

*

Fifteen sheep, their hind-feet

*

Libations offered by a liar

*

All the agreements in the world

*

The smallest of those stars is as large as the head of a man of middle
size

*

He makes himself guilty of the sin of breaking a man's leg

*

thwam khratus
[*Meaning unknown.*]

*

A place that gives pleasure, though not absolute pleasure

*

The column of life made marrowless

*

From there they come to kill and strike at heart, and they bring
locusts, as many as they want

*

The ox rose up, the land bore

*

Soon he changed this to death by the fault of his tongue

*

Of the same thickness

*

For the first time he comes near to her, for the first time he lies beside her

*

What is between the kidneys and the spleen?

*

The shortest *hathra* is of three words
[Hathra: *a measurement of both space and time.*]

*

The dead shall rise up, life shall come back to the bodies, and they shall keep the breath

*

The man who [. . .] does not [. . .] anything, be it ever so little

*

badha idha afrasani danhubyo
[*Meaning unknown.*]

*

It becomes more violent than that

*

Give lawful, well-examined woo

*

Another man, of a steady leg, [. . .] glory

*

stavano va puiti paidhi davaisne va
[*Meaning unknown.*]

*

Even uncovered and naked he will chant

*

How many sorts of plants are there?

*

If their fathers at once

*

In such a way that death should not be produced by burning

*

As much as a fly's wing, or of a wingless

*

He calls him

*

Let no man alone by himself carry a corpse

*

By two fingers, O holy Zarathustra!

*

Of the dog-kind

*

Than the nose is to the ears, or than the ears are to the mouth

*

For all of them shall a path be opened across the Kinvad bridge

*

As large as the top joint of the little finger

*

He has made the good waters and the good plants

*

And Paradise, boundless light, undeserved felicity

The Dead

It is not to honor the dead: it is to keep them from coming back. The heavy stones on the grave; the high walls and fences around cemeteries; the sturdy, well-sealed coffin. The dead, with hands and feet tied; the dead implored to stay where they are. The dying sent off somewhere else to die, so the dead won't linger in the house. Their eyes are closed, they are wrapped in a shroud so that they cannot see the way back. Circuitous paths to the graveyard; burials at night; masks on their faces that they cannot remove. A tiny house for them to live in, and stay there. Food and drink on the grave, the corpses dressed in fine clothes, money in the grave, so that they will not come back for more. A canoe or raft sent out to sea; the body burned to ashes; the body eaten by vultures. Loud noises, firecrackers, gongs, shouts, church bells ringing to frighten them away.

While the corpse is still in the house, one cannot eat, for it too will want to eat.

The name of the dead cannot be spoken, for it will think it is being called. The Abipones of the Gran Chaco had the given names of plants and animals. When one of them died, they had to invent something new in the language. The word for "jaguar," a common name, changed three or four times a year. By the end of the 19th century, there was no one left who spoke the language and could inadvertently summon the dead.

A Calendar of Stones

1

Each traveler, passing by, places a stone on the cairn.

2

Japan:

A rock on raked sand.

The shadow the rock casts.

3

Master Sheng Kung, the renowned Buddhist monk, preached by the side of a stream at the foot of Mount Hu-ch'iu. A thousand people attended, and none of them could understand what he was saying. But the unpolished stones, lying in the stream, rose up, bowed to him, and nodded in response.

4

The Aztec method for finding a precious stone:

Go out before dawn.

Face east.
As the sun rises, watch with diligence; do not blink.
A thin column of vapor will rise: the stone is there.
And if there is nothing lying on the ground, nothing visible, dig deep.

5

People are pebbles.

Deucalion and Pyrrha were the only ones to survive Zeus's wrathful flood. Lonely on earth, they sought the counsel of the goddess Themis, who told them to throw the bones of the Great Mother over their shoulders. Realizing that the bones of Mother Earth are rocks, they tossed stones. His became men, hers women.

Pebbles (*laas*), then, became people (*laos*).

6

A pair of 13th-century divines:

Meister Eckhart: "The stone is God, but does not know it, and it is the not knowing that makes it a stone."

Eckhart: "A stone also possesses love, and its love seeks the ground."

Mechthild of Magdeburg: "One day I saw with the eyes of my eternity in bliss and without effort, a stone. This stone was like a great mountain and was of assorted colors. It tasted sweet, like heavenly herbs. I asked the sweet stone: 'Who are you?' It replied: 'I am Jesus.'"

7

Yang produces heat and dryness; Yin produces cold and wet.

In the 5th century, there was a cave on the northeast side of a precipitous mountain in I-tu. You held a candle and went deep into the cave.

Inside were two large stones, ten feet apart, the Yin and the Yang.

In times of drought, you whipped the Yin Stone and the rains would come. In times of flood, you whipped the Yang Stone and the skies would clear.

However, the one who whipped the stone did not live long.

Wales:

The Thigh Stone—for it looked like a human thigh—could be carried away, but the next morning it would be back in its place. It was once tied with chains to a larger stone and thrown into the sea, and the next morning it was back in its place.

Stones that bring you gold; stones to remember everything; stones that expand and contract. Stones that won't let go of evil men; stones that cure rabies; a stone by the road that will give you a wart on your thumb if you happen to pick it up. The giants who had pebbles in their shoes that now are boulders. Stones that were once humans, paying for their sins.

Edgar the Peaceable banned the worship of stones.

The *Yogavasistha* is a massive poem from Kashmir, composed sometime between the 6th and 12th centuries, consisting of things left out of the *Ramayana*. One of the stories tells how the sage Vasistha, in a trance for a hundred years, meets a young and beautiful woman and goes with her to her home. At the end of the universe is the mountain Lokaloka (World-non-world); its peak is scattered with stones. The woman lives with her husband, an elderly brahmin, inside one of those stones, which is an entire universe. She complains that her husband imagined her into existence in order to have a wife as prescribed in the sacred texts, but he spends eternity studying the Vedas and is without passion. She is immortal, wasting her perpetual youth. He complains that she, trapped in the world of illusions and deep desires, has imagined him as her husband in a universe she has mentally created inside a stone. He says: "A man who is dreaming becomes a man in another man's dream." She says: "Our lives have no purpose."

10

In the Candomblé, the Orixás—Yoruba gods who are called "saints" in Brazil—are present in stones, the *otas*. An *ota* allows itself to be found by the priestess, the "mother of the saint," who washes it in blood or honey or palm oil or water mixed with sacred herbs, wraps it in cloth, places it in a pot or a dried calabash, and keeps it on an altar in an unlit, locked room. No one ever sees it. Food is left for it, and it is said that it grows inside its container.

One of these stones, seized in a raid in the 1920s when the authorities suppressed Candomblé, was briefly exhibited in a Police Museum, alongside confiscated weapons and photographs from autopsies. An anthropologist saw it: a greyish, somewhat round, nondescript rock.

Believers objected to its public exposure, and the *ota* was removed. But it could not be returned, for no one knew to which mother of the saint it had belonged. It is now somewhere in a police warehouse in Bahia, exerting its power.

11

Stones, said Thomas Nicols in the 17th century, can "make men rich and eloquent, preserve men from thunder and lightning, from plagues and disease, move dreams, procure sleep, foretell things to come, make men wise, strengthen memory, procure honors, hinder fascinations and witchcrafts, hinder slothfulness, put courage into men, keep men chaste, increase friendship, hinder difference and dissension, and make men invisible."

A dilemma: Stones can bring good luck, and yet some lead to misfortune. Why should this be so? Also in the 17th century, Anselmus de Boot, court physician to Rudolph II of Germany, explained that God sends angels to inhabit stones, to "guard men from dangers or to procure some special grace for them." However, the Devil can also "steal into the substance" of a stone, so that men become enamored with stones and forget God. This, he wrote, accounts for the particularly malevolent power of turquoise.

12

Cybele, the Anatolian earth goddess, loved black stones.

The only thing that Chinese immortals ate were white stones.

The caliphs of the Abbassid Dynasty believed their prestige was enhanced by red stones.

The Aka of northeast India venerate their ancestors, who inhabit yellow stones.

Sir Walter Raleigh claimed that Amazons, the warrior women of the Orinoco, would trade the Spaniards plates of gold for green stones.

It is said you'll sleep much better if you go to bed with blue stones.

When Orpheus played his flute, the stones arranged themselves around him.

13

Olaus Borrichius, in Copenhagen in the 17th century, reports:

"When precious stones are to be used in medicine, they must be pulverized until they are reduced to a powder so fine that it will not grate under the teeth, or, in the words of Galen, this powder must be as impalpable as 'that which is blown into the eyes.' Since this trituration is not usually operated with sufficient care by the apothecary, I begged a medical student, who was lodging with me, to pass an entire month in grinding some of these stones. I gave him emeralds, jacinths, sapphires, rubies, and pearls, an ounce of each kind. As these stones were rough and whole, he first crushed them a little in a well-polished iron mortar, using a pestle of the same metal; afterward he employed a pestle and mortar of glass, devoting several hours each day to this work. At the end of about three weeks, his room, which was rather large, became redolent with a perfume, agreeable both from its variety and sweetness. This odor, which much resembled that of March violets, lingered in the room for more than three days. There was nothing in the room to produce it, so that it certainly proceeded from the powder of precious stones."

14

Pseudo-Plutarch is the author of works attributed to Plutarch that are not by Plutarch; he may be one or more writers. His essay "On Rivers" is a minimalist compendium of nomenclature, violence, illicit sex, botany, and geology. In it, he cites works by Agatharchides, Archelaus, Aristobulus, Dercyllus, Dorotheus the Chaldean, Heracleitus, and Nicias of Mallus, all titled "On Stones." Doubt has been cast as to whether these texts, all lost, actually existed.

In the river Hydaspses, there is a luminescent, olive-colored stone called Lychnis, that may be found, when the moon waxes, by playing a flute.

In the river Pactolus, there is a stone called Aruraphylax. Lydians place it at the doors of their treasuries, for when thieves approach it emits a piercing trumpet-sound that follows the thieves until they fling themselves off the cliffs.

On Mount Tmolus nearby, is a stone that changes color four times a day, sought by virgins though seldom found, for it guards them against assault.

In the river Meander is a stone called Sophron. If you toss it into someone's lap, he becomes insane and murders his kin. Nearby, on Mount Sipylus, is its opposite: a stone that increases the love of sons for their fathers.

In the river Nile is a stone that resembles a bean. When dogs see it, they stop barking.

In the river Achelous is a stone called Lynurgus. Its desire for union is such, that if you throw it on a pile of linen, it turns the same color white.

15

The Kabbalists say the world was created with twenty-two letters, which are stones "quarried from the name of God." The *Sefer Yetzirah*, the *Book of Creation*, runs the permutations of the infinite variety of things that can be made from a finite number of elements:

"Two stones build two houses; three stones build six houses; four stones build twenty-four houses; five stones build a hundred and twenty houses; six stones build seven hundred and twenty houses; seven stones build five thousand and forty houses. Begin from there and think of what the mouth is unable to say and the ear unable to hear."

Beth-el, the "house of God," is a name for God and a name for sacred stones. Jacob, asleep on his pillow of twelve stones, which are the Twelve Tribes, dreams of angels climbing and descending a ladder to heaven. He sees the face of God, whom he thinks is the God of Abraham, and he names the place of his dream Bethel. The twelve stones have fused into one—one nation—in his sleep, and Jacob sets up the stone as an altar. But the citizens of Bethel believe there is another god named Bethel, and they worship him on Jacob's stone.

A stone is hard and endures; therefore it is in flux.

In Australia in March of 1887, Mr. and Mrs. Large and their fifteen children, living on a remote farm whose nearest town was Mudgee, reported to the police that black stones, some weighing as much as a pound, were falling inside their house, landing with a dull thud. They appeared to come through the roof, but without causing damage to the roof.

This continued nightly, and hundreds came from around the district to witness the spectacle. A local newspaper noted that "as soon as the stones fall the children of the house pick them up and hand them over to the visitors with feelings of awe." One of the visitors was quoted: "It is an easy matter to convince superstitious people that alleged occurrences are facts, but when sceptics go and see and sit with the woman and her husband in the same room, and have stones dropping round about them they are very glad to be rid of such unpleasant associations." The police could find no explanation, and the family eventually abandoned the farm.

17

Also near Mudgee is a town called St. Fillans.

St. Fillan, in the 8th century, was born with a stone in his mouth, like Pao Yu, the hero of *The Story of the Stone*. His father, an Irish prince, was terrified and threw the baby in a lake. A passing priest rescued him; his mother, in gratitude, converted to Christianity and they moved to Scotland. Fillan became a monk. His left hand and arm radiated light, so that he could read the Scriptures in the dark. He miraculously cured the mentally ill. A thousand years later, the mad were still tied up, dunked in a pool of water next to the ruins of his abbey and left overnight.

In Killin, where he is honored, they have nine river stones that he blessed. Each one is effective for a different part of the body. They are taken out once a year on Christmas Eve and placed on a bed of straw. Parishioners pick up the appropriate stone and rub it on the place that ails them.

18

An icon of Brazilian modernism, their red wheelbarrow, Carlos Drummond de Andrade's poem from 1930:

> IN THE MIDDLE OF THE ROAD
> In the middle of the road there was a stone.
> There was a stone in the middle of the road.
> There was a stone.
> In the middle of the road there was a stone.
>
> I'll never forget this
> All my life of tired eyes.
> I'll never forget that in the middle of the road
> There was a stone.
>
> There was a stone in the middle of the road
> In the middle of the road there was a stone.

19

A cairn is a gate or a ladder to heaven.

Herma, a heap of stones at a crossroads or boundary, becomes Hermes, the trickster god of countless attributes, and a rectangular stone with a head and a phallus, sometimes with a bearded Hermes, sometimes with Athena (the hermathena), sometimes with Aphrodite (the hermaphrodite). Hermes the messenger, the liaison between the world of the gods and the world of people.

In the early Christian centuries, Hermes combines with the Egyptian god Thoth to become the Thrice-Greatest, Hermes Trismegistus, master of astrology, alchemy, and magic; the solitary sage; the hermit who preached the oneness of god and the universe; a kind of saint for the heretics of the Renaissance, the hermeticists. "As above, so below": male is female, lead is gold, the stones of gods are the pebbles of people.

20

An incantation from Assyria:

> The splendid stones! The splendid stones! The stones of
>   abundance and of joy,
> Made resplendent for the flesh of the gods.
> The *hulalini* stone, the *sirgarru* stone, the *hulalu* stone, the
>   *sundu* stone, the *uknu* stone.
> The *dushu* stone, the precious stone *elmeshu* perfect in celestial
>   beauty.
> The stone of which the *pingu*, the pendant, is set in gold,
> Placed on the shining breast of the king.
> Azagsud, high priest of Bel, make them shine, make them
>   sparkle!

Three thousand years later, it is no longer known which stones these are; the rocks have drifted from their names.

21

According to the Teton Sioux shaman, Lone Man, "This earth is under the protection of something that at times becomes visible to the eye. One would think that this would be at the center of the earth, but its representations appear everywhere, in large and small forms. They are the sacred stones."

In the 19th century, Bear Necklace was on a buffalo hunt and fell from his horse onto a pile of stones. When he awoke, he said that all rocks and stones "were people turned to stone." He became a "dreamer of stones," which he could make fly through the air, and which told him where to find buffalo or lost horses, when war parties were coming, and who had been killed in a far-off raid. Sitting Bull asked the stones to make him famous, and Bear Necklace gave him a stone that he wore around his neck until he died; he was buried with it.

22

Bear Necklace gave this song to his son, Charging Thunder:

> Someone somewhere
> is speaking
> From the North
> a Sacred-Stone Nation
> is speaking
> You will hear
> someone somewhere
> speaking

Cherokee shamans could cause a man's death by burying seven earthworms and seven yellow stones.

23

The Irish saint Columba slept, like Jacob, on a stone pillow. It became his gravestone. His dreams are not recorded.

He took a pebble out of the River Nessa and said: "Behold this white pebble by which God will effect the cure of many diseases among this heathen nation."

It was true. Placed in a glass of water, it floated like a nut and could not be submerged; it cured the maladies of many people. And yet, writes St. Adamnan, Ninth Abbot of the Monastery of Iona, "what is very wonderful, when this same stone was sought for by those sick persons whose term of life had arrived, it could not be found."

24

A stone is impermeable; therefore it is inhabited by spirits, souls, and ghosts.

A stone is dry; therefore, dipped in a river or sprinkled with water, it brings rain.

A stone is lifeless; therefore it brings life. Stones are tied to the branches of fruit trees; stones are buried in fields; stones are rubbed on the bellies of women.

Eckhart: "A stone is never free of motion as long as it is not on the ground."

25

Han Yu, the Tang Dynasty poet, explains:

"There are some things that have form but no sound, such as stones; others have sound but no form, such as the wind or thunder; others have both sound and form, such as people and animals; and finally there is a category of things that have neither sound nor form, such as ghosts."

26

Japan:

A stranger hands you a stone and asks you to hold it.
Puzzled, you take it.
The stone grows.
And grows until you are crushed.

27

The Jains say that, in every stone on the road, a soul is trapped in a prison of silent suffering. In this incarnation, its pain is greater than that of seemingly sentient beings, for it is so tightly enclosed by matter that it cannot move nor cry out in pain when kicked by an oblivious foot.

28

D. H. Lawrence on the moon:

"It's no use telling me it's a dead rock in the sky! I *know* it's not."

The Frog Groom

Each year, in the village of Pullipudupet, in southern India, a very young girl is selected to marry a frog. The customs of a traditional Indian wedding are followed. Half the village becomes the bride's family, and half the groom's. Accompanied by a marching band, the groom is led on a white horse to be welcomed at the bride's home. The entire nuptial ceremony is performed: the couple circles the sacred fire seven times; the edge of the bride's sari is tied to the groom's sash; their heads are held together by the priest. After the wedding banquet, the frog is released in a pond. The bride returns to her life as a schoolgirl. When she grows up, she is free to take a second, human husband.

An Indian journalist visited Pullipudupet to witness the ceremony. He asked the villagers why, each year, they marry a very young girl to a frog. No one knew; it was just what they had always done.

The Mara

The Mara, in northeast India, say that ordinary mortals, when they die, go to Athiki, the village of the dead. There it is night when it is day here, and day when it is night. Fish are bamboo leaves there, and bears are hairy caterpillars. The spirit lives for a long time in Athiki, but ultimately dies and comes back to earth. The spirit of a powerful person turns into a bit of heat mist that rises into the sky. The spirit of a poor person becomes a worm and is eaten by a chicken.

They say that when people dream, their souls wander off at the end of a long invisible string. When they have a bad dream, they tell everyone about it. When they have a good dream, they keep it to themselves.

They say that there is a giant ficus tree growing on the moon, and the marks on the moon's face that we see are its branches. Living in the tree is a headless monkey.

The greatest hunters go forever to paradise, called Peira. It is close to the one God and occupied by few, for one must have killed a man in battle, an elephant, a tiger, a bear, a small tree bear, a serow, a gural, a mithun, a rhinoceros, a sambhur, a barking deer, a wild boar, a crocodile, a hamadryad, an eagle, one of each of the kinds of hornbill, and a king crow. Government troops now keep the peace, and many of the animals are no longer there, so it is unlikely that any Mara will ever go to paradise again.

The Lushei

The Lushei, neighbors of the Mara, believe that earthquakes are caused by the people who live in the lower world shaking the ground to see if anyone is still alive up there. When an earthquake occurs, the Lushei run out of their houses and shout "Alive! Alive!" so that those below will know, and stop the shaking.

Changs Dreaming

It was recorded in the 14th century, in the *History of the Sung Dynasty*, that the Empress Chang-i dreamed that there were two suns in the sky, that one of them fell and that she caught it with the front of her gown. It was also recorded that she dreamed that someone barefoot, dressed in feathers, came through her window.

It was recorded in the 10th century, in *Elegant Chats from a Commandery Studio*, that Chang Chiung was unable to write poetry. He dreamed that a many-colored cloud came down from the sky, and that he grabbed a piece and ate it. It was noted that he became a master poet.

It was recorded in the 7th century, in the *History of the Chin Dynasty*, that Mistress Chang dreamed that the sun entered her body. It was noted that she was pregnant for fifteen months.

It was also recorded in the *History of the Chin Dynasty* that Assistant Magistrate Chang Chai dreamed that he rode up a mountain, seeing only junipers and pines, and that he circled a house three times but could not find the door. It was recorded that a scholar explained that junipers and pines surround a tomb, and therefore he could not find the door because there was no door; three times meant three years. It was noted that three years later Chang Chai was involved in a rebellious conspiracy and was executed.

It was recorded in the 10th century, in the *Old History of the Tang Dynasty*, that Chang Chih-ho's mother became pregnant when she dreamed that a maple tree was growing from her stomach, that Chang Yueh's mother became pregnant when she dreamed that a jade swallow flew in from the southwest and entered her body, and that Chang Chiu-ling's mother became pregnant when she dreamed that nine cranes came down from the sky and gathered in the courtyard of her house. It was noted that the boy was named Chiu-ling, which means "nine extra years."

It was recorded in the 12th century, in the *Collected Stories of Anomalies*, that Chang T'ien-hsi dreamed that a green dog with a long body came from the south and tried to bite him.

It was recorded in the 7th century, in the *Encyclopedia for Literary Composition*, that the wife of Chang Huan, governor of Wu-wei, dreamed that she was wearing her husband's official seal, climbed up a tower, and began to sing.

It was recorded in the 10th century, in *The T'ai-p'ing Miscellany*, that Chang Cho, a student, dreamed that his body was covered with clouds. It was noted that he received first place in the examinations.

It was also recorded in *The T'ai-p'ing Miscellany*, that Chang Shen-t'ung dreamed that another ear grew on his head. It was noted that he became known as the "Three-Eared Scholar."

It was recorded in the 11th century, in *A Record of Inner Light*, that Rectifier Chang became gravely ill and dreamed that he was pregnant. It was noted that this repelled him.

It was recorded in the 6th century, in the *History of the Southern Ch'i Dynasty*, that Chang Ching'er's wife told him: "A long time ago I dreamed my hands were as hot as fire, and you became Administrator of Nan-yang Commandery. Then I dreamed that half my body was as hot as fire and you became Magistrate of Hsiang-yang. Last night I dreamed that my entire body was as hot as fire." It was recorded that a eunuch overheard the conversation and reported it to the Emperor, and it was noted that, a few days later, Chang Ching'er was executed.

It was recorded in the 9th century, in *A Collection of Strange Tales*, that Chang Ju-ming was a filial son whose grief at his parent's death was such, he became thin and weak and would stumble when walking. It was recorded that he dreamed that his father taught him the method of ingesting the Southern Star. It was noted that he then regained his health.

It was recorded in the 9th century, in *Miscellaneous Morsels from Yu-yang*, that Chang Chan was away from home and dreamed that he was cooking in a stone mortar. It was noted that a scholar told him it meant that he would never see his wife again.

It was also recorded in *Miscellaneous Morsels from Yu-yang*, that Chang Hsing-kung, the son of Magistrate Chang T'ing, had a dream after his father died. His friend, Chang Ch'ui, appeared and presented him with a poem that read:

> Misery, misery, and more misery.
> This hall in autumn seems a hundred years old.
> It's the Cold Meal Festival and I'm all alone,
> Far off in nowhere.

It was noted that Chang Hsing-kung was startled awake, and died a few days later.

It was recorded in the 10th century, in *Master Wang's Record of Things Heard and Seen*, that Chang Wen-i, whenever he left the city, would visit an old monk. Although Chang Wen-i arrived unannounced, the monk would always be waiting for him at the gate to the temple. Chang Wen-i wondered how this was possible. The monk told him:

"I dream that the god of the mountain tells me that a future Grand Councilor will be arriving the next day."

One day the monk did not appear. He explained that the god did not inform him of the visit. Chang Wen-i asked the monk to find out why. That night the monk dreamed that the god of the mountain told him that Chang Wen-i had unfairly judged a case concerning the killing of an ox, and that he will never be a Grand Councilor.

Chang Wen-i remembered that there had indeed been such a case, and he reversed his decision. It was recorded that the next time he visited the temple, the monk was there waiting at the gate. He explained that last night, in his dreams, the god of the mountain had told him that Chang Wen-i had been reinstated as a future Grand Councilor. His life, however, had been shortened.

It was recorded in the 12th century, in *The Valley Embroidered with Myriad Flowers*, that Lady Chang dreamed that a Taoist priest named Mountain Dweller with a Heart of Jade appeared to her and asked her help with his rebirth. Soon after, she gave birth to a crane. The family was alarmed and threw the chick into the river. It was recorded that Lady Chang's uncle intervened: "I have heard that the births of extraordinary men who appear between long intervals are always unusual." The family rushed to the river and found a child covered with feathers. It was noted that, a month later, the feathers fell off.

It was recorded in the 8th century, in the *Collected Records of Court and Countryside*, that Chang Cho dreamed that he was wearing a crimson robe and riding a donkey. He could not understand why, wearing the robes of a minister, he was not riding a horse.

It was recorded in the 3rd century BCE, in the *Han Fei Tzu*, that Chang Min and Kao Hui were friends, but lived far apart and rarely met, and that Chang went to find Kao in a dream, but halfway there became lost.

A Journey on the River Amazon

[1849]

the shrill stridulation of a vast number of field crickets
the plaintive hooting of tree frogs
this uproar of life never ceases

I saw for the first time the sky-blue Chatterer
a quiet bird

The Ghosts of Birds

In the storm, along the cliff-face,
                                    they perch, hover, twisted, fall:
                                                        the birds
calling their own names:

                    Keeea cries the kea,
                                        riroriro says the riroriro,
                    Koekoeeeeeā chants the koekoeā,
                    the long-tailed cuckoo,
                    who sings only when the wind is from the north or west.

        Aloft, floating:
                                birds in "a space that no one's ever seen."

The sharp-eyed miromiro, who brings back errant wives and husbands,
who must be captured and then released for the sweet potatoes to
    flourish.

                    The karuwai, with its watery eyes,
                    who could predict success or failure in battle.
                    Its song at dawn could revive a dying man.

The kērangi, the harrier, the child of the goddess of fire;
its small red feathers the seeds of flame.
Kē kē kē is its call and *rangi* the heavens.
Kērangi: a sound in the sky.

                    Birds in the storm clouds.
                    Birds in the stars of the Southern Cross.

75

The toroa, the albatross, "long and gliding."
Its whiteness comes from the heaven of light.
"When fog descends, the toroa thinks only of home."
Why does it spend so much time on the sea?

The kōtuko, the white heron, who is seen only once in a lifetime.
Its rareness, its whiteness, provoke lamentation and respect.

"The great albatross has flown off on the wind,
       the great albatross has flown,
    leaving me with white heron feathers in my hair."

                                    There they scurry,
                                    they dart:

The mātātā, the fernbird, who can barely fly.

            The land-locked kākāpō,
            the parrot of the night,
            the "hidden bird" who tells the future.

The kōkako, the crow, who brought Maui water, and Maui rewarded it
with long legs so it could walk through mud and water and not get wet.
It says:
     whio who whio who
                     and sounds like people talking.

            A kiwi crying *ki-wi*.
            It can hear the sounds of worms moving in the earth.

            (A weka,
                    patiently waits for the kiwi

to find the food it steals.)

A kiwi startled,
                    stops still,
                                    curls up,
itself looks like a lump of earth,
                                    and disappears.

They dart:

    The tiny tītitipounamu, a messenger of the gods,
    whose name means "a vision of green jade,"
    and the British saw as the "rifleman,"
    for its color matched the uniforms of the Rifle Brigade.

    The tūī, guardian of the sacred number twelve,
    who was trained to talk, syllable by syllable,
        by altering its tongue and throat
            until it could repeat
songs, prayers, proverbs, genealogies, and words of welcome.

        Tūī means "to fasten" or "sew."
        Its song ties heaven to earth.

                They perch:

    The pīpīwharauroa,
    the migratory shining cuckoo,
    the "little bird of the long journey,"
        the harbinger of spring.
Its name is the name of a thin cloud that stretches across the sky.
        It holds a pebble in its mouth

to slake its thirst
as it flies from Indonesia.
It calls out *whitti whitti ora*,
"safely, safely crossed, alive."

The birds in the cliff-face.
The faces in the cliff-face.

The kōkōmako, whom Captain Cook named the bellbird;
its song, said Joseph Banks, is "like small bells exquisitely tuned."
It too carries messages from and to the gods.
 The day begins when it sings:
"Matariki is a star"
                    (a star in the Pleiades)
                              "but I am but a small bellbird."

Fluttering:

The hīwaiwaka, the tīrairaka, the tīwakawaka, the tītakataka,
all the names of the fantail, the flycatcher,
the bird that never rests.

Ko Tāne mata nui:
Tāne can see all you do,
for he is a god and the birds are his eyes.

Fluttering, twittering:

Parakeets   parakeets   parakeets.

Young girls would paint themselves like parakeets.

Bothersome children are like parakeets.
If you dream a parakeet is lying in an oven
            you may be certain that soon you will die.
The shells of hatched parakeets turn into maggots,
                                          which turn into lizards,
which creep down the throats of sleeping people.

            Parakeets:
            Kākāriki, the red-crowned parakeet,
            who had his head splashed with blood
            when Māui killed the eel monster Tunarua.

Red: the color of bravery. Red: the sacred color of the gods. Red
feathers on the cloaks, mats, axes, kites, headdresses, digging sticks,
the gables of houses, the ceremonial aprons. Red feathers tied to the
middle finger of the corpse of a chief.

There were ninety shades of red. Red feathers were said to shine in
      darkness.
Red shift: it shifts to red as it retreats in distance and time . . .

Perched:
            Hovering:
                        They
                              "dwelleth and abideth on the rock,
                              upon the crag of the rock."

            Taiāmai: a place and a bird.
            The bird escaped capture by melting into a rock.
            The place is the land around the rock.

"The pūriri trees of Taiāmai are laughing."

Taiāmai means "toward us from the sea."
"Its name is Taiāmai; it exists, it exists."

Fluttering:

> *Ka ngaro reoreo tangata, kīkī e manu.*
> No human voice was heard, only the twittering of the birds.

The conference of the birds:
"You're a sly one; you're a beggar; you're a parasite; you're a king-
     fisher."
"Greetings to you, a white heron sitting by the river at the setting
     sun."
"I shall die in my nest."
"Pigeons are like a lot of eels on a stick."
"Ducks are gluttons."
"A bearded man is cause for a cormorant to vomit."
"He who scales cliffs will die by the cliff."
"My legs are always adorned with red feathers:
         They treat me well wherever I go."
"Hiwa! Kia hiwa!" "Be alert! Be very alert!"

                              Floating, aloft, falling
                              through the space
                              "no one's ever seen":
                              the ghosts of birds.

For the cormorants of the open sea and the cormorants of the rivers
and the lakes started a war of all the birds over whose fishing grounds
were superior. The sea birds were stronger, the land birds more clever,
and the land birds won.

A red-billed gull, tarāpunga,
                              seen inland,
          is looking for the bodies of his dead comrades.

"O thou that dwellest in the clefts of the rock,
that holdest the height of the hill:
though thou shouldst make thy nest as high as the eagle,
I will bring thee down."

      The birds of ghosts,
                    the ghosts of birds,
                              calling their own names:

          The koukou, the Morepork owl, hoots *koukou*.
          It lives by night, it belongs to the Underworld,
          its frightening eyes a sign of evil.
          A thin film covers its unblinking eyes,
          a thin film made from the fingernails of corpses.

The tīeke, the saddleback, cries *tīeke-tīeke*.
Its voice is the spirit of a dead warrior,
warning those who would trespass in his territory.
                    It guards over treasures
                    and a great stone called Taininihi,
                         that could move on its own from place to place.

          Hū hū hū murmurs the matuku, the bittern,
          as it stands still for hours,
                              pretending it is not there.
          They say those sounds are the cries of heavenly beings
          who have come to earth
                              and cannot find their way home.

(Miromiro feathers in the hair of the dead.)

They say, in the war with the white people, an old woman was left to
guard the village. She sang:

> "No sound, no cry,
> but the tītī calling in the dark,
> calling as they go by.
> They fly in pairs, but I'm alone,
> alone like the kiwi's solitary egg,
> left in the roots of the tawai trees.
> Three trees above my head,
> and I an egg left hidden in the roots."

Kōtare, the kingfisher, was perched above a tūī singing sweetly in the
trees. The kingfisher dived, pierced the tūī's skull and let it fall dead
to the ground. Then it flew away.

The ghosts of birds:
                    No rain falls:
                              Thunder:
                                        Birds crash on the cliff-face.
The ghosts:

The koreke, the "treasure bird," the "bird of signs," brought down
from heaven by Tāwhaki so that its feathers could adorn his wife—a
quail now extinct.

The whēkau, the laughing owl, who lived in deep holes in those cliffs.
It vanished a century ago, stung to death by imported bees. It didn't
laugh, it shrieked.

The solitary takahē, called Moho the Hermit, who disappeared for decades and then appeared again, no one knew from where.

The hōkioi, extinct for centuries, who sang *hōkioi, hōkioi*. But at night on the eve of battle, it would screech *kakao, kakao*—the sound it made choking on the hair of the heads of the warriors who would die the next day.

They plummet, twisted backwards:

The beautiful huia was a celestial bird. It guarded the door to the twelfth heaven; its twelve tail feathers the twelve months and twelve periods of darkness and twelve stages of gestation before a child is born. A single feather could ward off bad luck.

The male with its short beak fed the female with her long beak; she
    did not feed him.
They were inseparable, and one did not long outlive the other.
They were too trusting of humans and vanished in 1907.

The ghosts:

The piopio, whose song *piopio* will never be heard again.

The toroa, the albatross, forever at sea, for a man and his wife could not stop arguing, so the gods turned him into an albatross, and condemned him to wander the endless sea. His wife became a tree fern and in shame she let her long hair fall in front of her face, and these are the long fronds swaying in the wind.

The riroriro sings *riiiiiiro riro riro riro riro*, "gone, gone, gone, gone."

83

"We are like the cormorant sitting on a rock.
The tide rises, flows over the rock, and it flies away.
We have no dry resting place."

"Gone, gone."

"And I saw an angel standing in the sun,
who cried in a loud voice to all the birds flying in midair."

Perched, hovering, twisted backward, falling:

"Flying birds like sand on the seashore"
and a kūaka that lands,
"a single bird that imprints the dune"

and its tracks wrote:

Taiāmai
a rock
a bird
"toward us from the sea"
"it exists, it exists"

Ou-yang Hsiu's Fu *on the Sound of Autumn*
[1069]

Sent to a post in the far northeast, I, Ou-yang Hsiu, was studying
    my books by lamplight.

Cold winds come from the north, the winds that bring rain come from
    the east, but I heard the rumors of a sound from the southwest.

I listened in trepidation. I said to myself "how strange."

First, a soft breeze, a light rain, then suddenly the sound of rushing,
    of huge stones colliding, of waves crashing.

The sound of water gushing, an alarm spreading through the night,
    wind and rain pushing toward some finality.

Drumbeats, bells ringing, iron clanging against gold, everything in
    harm's way.

And a low sound of soldiers hurrying to the siege: the hooves of the
    horses muffled, no orders shouted, just a steady tramping for-
    ward.

I told the boy: "What is that sound? Go out and see."

The boy said:

"The stars and moon are clear and bright. The Milky Way lies across
    the sky. On all four sides no sound of people. The only sound is
    in the trees."

I said: "How sad.

It is the sound of autumn. Why does autumn ever come?

Autumn is pale and cruel. Smoke rises, clouds gather.

Even when skies are bright, autumn is bitter, piercing flesh and
    piercing bone.

Everything is alone: the world of mountains and rivers becomes
    empty and still.

The sound of autumn is cold. It is the sound of grief, the sound of
   sudden wailing.

"Once there were the delicate patterns of thick grass.
Once there was green shade lying under the trees.

"Autumn touches the grass and its color fades. Autumn touches the
   trees and the leaves fall.
It cannot help but destroy. Its nature is corrosive.
Its occupation is executioner. Its badge is darkness.
Its color may be gold, but its sword is steel.
It is the pitiless justice of heaven and earth: to kill with cold.

"The sound of autumn is a flute sound, a sad song, the sound of
   things being hurt, the sound of things past their prime that will
   soon be put to death.

"Trees and grass don't care. The moment arrives, the wind changes,
   and they die.
But a man thinks, his heart aches, the endless things wear him down.
He is adrift and yet—the sperm still rises.
He craves that which is unreachable.
He imagines spreading his wisdom among the impractical.

"His bright face has turned to dead wood, his black hair white as
   stars.
We are not made of metal and stone, why should we dream of out-
   lasting the trees and grass?
Why should we hate the sound of autumn?"

The boy did not answer. He had fallen asleep.
Inside the four walls I could hear the *chrrr...chrrr...* of insects
   gnawing.

Winter
[1827]

Deer tracks in the snowy meadow.

Twisted tree shadows cast by the moon.

I was a stranger; she spoke of love.

I stop by her gate and write "Gute Nacht" in the snow.

The weathervane turns this way and that in the gusts of wind.

My hat flies off my head.

My hair is still black and is white from snow.

There is a linden by the fountain at her gate.

She has left no footprints in the snow.

One leaf hangs from the linden.

I watch the leaf turning in the gusts of wind.

Dogs bark, people sleep, dreaming of what they never did.

A crow flies around my head.

The postman will bring no letters.

William Sharpe

Pascal said that all of man's problems come from the inability to remain in one room. The life of William Sharpe, who lived on a farm called "The Worlds" near the village of Keighley in Yorkshire, and died on March 3, 1856, would be, then, exemplary.

Sharpe, the son of a prosperous weaver and notorious skinflint, spent much of his time in the local pub. He fell in love with the pretty barmaid there, proposed and was accepted. But on the day of his marriage in Keighley Church, his father refused to settle any money on the couple and the bride's father, in a rage, tore up the certificate.

Sharpe took to his bed. He was thirty years old, and stayed there for the next forty-nine years. The room was nine feet by nine feet, with a cold and damp, uncovered stone floor and a fireplace that could only be lit on the days when the wind blew in a certain direction. The single window was not opened for the last thirty-eight of those years. The only furnishings were the bed, a small oak table, and—although it seems too perfect—a grandfather clock that had neither pendulum nor weights, and was covered with cobwebs.

He lay naked in the bed and refused to speak. When someone entered the room, he would hide under the sheets. Thanks ultimately to a bequest from his father, he was well-maintained and fed, and was in perfect health throughout his life, though he grew obese and his legs atrophied and bent backward. At his funeral, attended by crowds of the curious, the coffin was a cube and weighed 480 pounds.

Someone once spied through the window and saw him spinning his dinner plate on his finger, in the manner of a Chinese juggler. But he was apparently not without problems. On the last day of his life, he finally spoke again. He said: "Poor Bill! Poor Bill! Poor Bill Sharpe!"

II.

II

The Great Wall

Richard Nixon, visiting the Great Wall of China in 1972, said: "I think you would have to conclude that this is a great wall."

Ronald Reagan, visiting the Wall in 1984, said: "What can you say, except it's awe-inspiring? It is one of the great wonders of the world." Asked if he would like to build his own Great Wall, Reagan drew a circle in the air and replied: "Around the White House."

Bill Clinton, visiting the Wall in 1998, said: "So if we had a couple of hours, we could walk ten kilometers, and we'd hit the steepest incline, and we'd all be in very good shape when we finished. Or we'd be finished. It was a good workout. It was great."

George W. Bush, visiting the Wall in 2002, signed the guest book and said: "Let's go home." He made no other comments.

Barack Obama, visiting the Wall in 2009, said: "It's majestic. It's magical. It reminds you of the sweep of history, and that our time here on Earth is not that long, so we better make the best of it." During his visit, the Starbucks and KFC at the base of the Wall were closed.

The City

[A few blocks]

In the beginning, or one of the beginnings, the village. The Santals, an indigenous people living in the forest in the state of Bihar, in India, have a song that goes, in its entirety:

> In the trees the birds are singing.
> In the village the girls are singing.

An image of untroubled tranquility, humankind and nature in cosmic harmony. The girls sing and the birds sing. And even more: They sing to each other.

*

In the beginning, or one of the beginnings, the city was not a mercantile center or even a military fortress. It was created by an authoritarian power as an expression of cosmic power, and built in the image of the cosmos itself. The city was the navel of the world, or the axis of the world, perfectly aligned (or, in Mesoamerica, deliberately slightly misaligned, for humans are imperfect) to the four directions. At its center was a raised structure—tower, ziggurat, temple, platform, pyramid, palace—where one could be even closer to the gods, so that the gods could better hear the human prayers, and the humans hear the divine instructions. And directly below the city was another city, the underworld, city of the dead.

The Babylonian cities were each modeled on a constellation: Nineveh on Ursa Major, Sippar on Cancer, Assur on Arcturus, Babylon on Cetus-

Aires. The Han capital of Ch'ang-an was laid out in the pattern of the Big and Little Dippers combined, with the imperial palace at the Pole Star; the city of Hsien-yang according to the stars in the constellations we call Cassiopeia and Pegasus. The first Khmer capital, Yasodharapura, was itself a calendar, with 108 towers representing the four phases of the moon and the twenty-seven lunar mansions, and sixty towers arranged in five sets of twelve that was the twelve-year cycle of Jupiter with which, in multiples of five, the Khmers measured historical eras. The city was not the macrocosm of a village, but the microcosm of the universe.

Cities were never new. Whether in Mesopotamia or Egypt or China, the ruler justified the construction of his city by stating that the design copied one handed down from the ancestors. In the 5th century BCE, a poem in the first Chinese anthology, the *Shi Ching*, the *Book of Odes* or *Songs*, sings the praises of King Wen, who had built the city of Feng, six hundred years before: "He made Feng according to the ancient plan. / He did not fulfill his own desires, / But worked in pious obedience to the dead." Creation, in cyclical time, is always re-creation. The city—our model of novelty and modernity—was their model of antiquity. The city—our model of change—was their model of stasis. The city—our model of unfettered life—was ruled by the dead. In the 1930s, Thomas Wolfe wrote a short story with a matchless title: "Only the Dead Know Brooklyn."

Our cities are full of stories. Their cities were themselves stories. The Inka capital of Cusco, which was in the shape of a jaguar, was organized in a net of invisible lines, connected by natural and artificial markers (*huacas*), with each line a songline to be followed, a mnemonic device for retelling their myths and histories. Around the central tower in Yasodharapura, which represented Mt. Meru, home of the gods, the 108 towers were arranged so that, from the middle point of any side, only thirty-three could be seen—the homes of the thirty-three gods of Indra's heaven. From each of the cardinal points, only three of the five tallest towers could be seen: the three peaks of Mt. Meru, which are the heavenly cities of Vishnu, Brahma, and Shiva. The city was a map of a narrative.

Cities that feared no earthly enemies were laid out in grid patterns; those in disputed territory were labyrinths of alleyways and plazas, where an invading army would get lost and be defeated. Whether grid or labyrinth, cities were walled, for they were fortresses of cosmic power in a struggle against other powers: demons, the evil gods, the angry ghosts of the human dead. The city wall was magical before it was military, marking a place of order in the chaos of the world. Royal genealogies began with the date of the erection of the city walls—the establishment of the new order. Periodic mass circumambulations were celebrated, and special ones in times of disaster, drought, plague: a communal reassertion of who we are, where we are, what is our place in the world.

All were strictly compartmentalized: sacred zones; markets arranged by the goods sold and the services offered; residential districts for the rich, the poor, the merchants, or organized by clan; pleasure quarters, and so on. Cities were aggregates of villages, like villages in their daily life of familiarity and local interactions, but unlike villages in their specialization of class or task, and in their subservience to a higher power. Cities were hierarchical, as villages were not. The best metaphor for the ancient city is the skyscraper—boxes, horizontal in actual space, but metaphorically piled one on another by social rank, reaching to the gods of the sky—millennia before skyscrapers were constructed.

*

The ancient city was an emblem of order in the chaos of the world, particularly the dangerous chaos of the natural world, with its dark forests, wild men, hungry beasts and hungry ghosts. With the simultaneous, and not coincidental, rise of both Romanticism and the industrial city, the images reversed: The natural world was one of tranquility and order; the city was pandemonium.

The literature of the city—nearly, but not all, modern literature—is panoramic, sometimes celebratory, often horror-struck: the hubbub of voices speaking different languages or dialects, the conglomeration of apprehended fragments. Its medium is the collage; its science that opposites attract; its logic that every proposition and its converse are equally true.

The modern city, it is often said, is built on anonymity. Its local goddess is Baudelaire's passerby, its act of devotion what Walter Benjamin called the quintessential urban experience: "love at last sight." Its mythic hero is the detective, the man who must find the name of the anonymous perpetrator of the crime.

But the modern city is, or was, as is less often said, a collection of neighborhoods. In the neighborhood, not all the names are known, but the faces are familiar. The stereotypical anonymity of the modern city is in its mercantile districts, or on its transportation, or in someone else's neighborhood. Even speech was once narrowly local: In my city, New York, neighborhoods—except for the very poor—tended to be organized more by ethnicity than class. In my childhood, each still retained an identifiable way of speaking. Air-conditioning erased that sense of community, keeping everyone indoors in the summer, off the streets and in their own apartments—watching television, that overwhelming homogenizer of language.

The literature of the neighborhood was the vignette—one story or image from the millions of stories or images. (Or, in the case of Dos Passos and Bely and Döblin and others, a panorama made from many vignettes.) The poet picks out a detail, as lyric poets have always done. The fiction writer tells the tale of a few characters, as has always been told. Their fates may be senseless and cruel; their fates may no longer be determined by the gods; but their fates remain narrative conclusions (or inconclusions). If the city is chaos, the neighborhood, whether lives are happy or miserable, has a kind of order.

*

The literature of the city was something new, in both form and content: the modernity of modern literature and the visual arts. The literature of the neighborhood was the antiquity within that modernity. But now something has happened to the city, largely in the Third World, as migrants from the countryside flood in, and metropolis becomes megalopolis. Except at the extremes of rich and poor, the neighborhood—the sense of the neighborhood—has vanished in the endless repetition of colorless apartment blocks, large or small. Many of the major cities are now nowhere. One inhabits a random spot identical to a million other random spots. In the megalopolis there is no place in the world, and community, as one longs for community, tends to be found in the structured societies of religion and ideological politics, or in the ad hoc networks of cyberspace.

The literature of the neighborhood is still being written in the last neighborhoods—the penthouses or the slums. But what will be the literature of the megalopolis? Already late modernism, so-called postmodernism, is perhaps pointing the way: the novel that is short on memorable characters or compelling narrative, long on pyrotechnical wordplay and a glut of information; the poem that is a string of disconnected ironies and pastiches of appropriated language. A literature with everyone and no one, a literature where—as is said of the slightly crazed—"there's nobody home." I suspect that those of us raised in the modern city, and raised on modernism, won't understand it at all.

The emptying villages; the cities that have become concentrated suburbs, where life unfolds beside the driveway or the parking lot; the cities that are theme parks devoted to their former glories, its citizens serving the gawkers; the shipwrecked cities of abandoned factories; the robot cities of the "new economic zones"; the three or four or five cities that still retain their vivacity, breathing the old-fashioned cosmopolitanism devoted to the new; and then, the megalopolis. This century, much of humanity will be adrift in the megalopolis—or, more exactly, stuck in its traffic. It remains to be seen how humanity will reinvent its humanness in the least human environment humans have invented.

[2009]

The Wall

1

At 8:46 p.m. at Rudower Höhe, the sentry sneezed and a West Berlin customs officer shouted back, "Gesundheit!"

At 11:40 a.m. at the Kiesberg sentry post, three West Berlin youths shouted: "Hey, guys, still smoking rags? Want an HB cigarette? Come over and get one."

At 9:25 a.m. at the Buckersberg sentry post, two men, aged thirty-five to forty, asked: "Did you see two children yesterday afternoon, riding their bicycles along the canal?" At 5:50 p.m., the fire department arrived and two divers went into the canal. At 6:50 p.m., they left, having found nothing.

At 12:19 p.m. at the Teltowkanal, a man about thirty years old called out: "I hope this shit ends soon, so we can be friends again."

At 1:15 p.m. at the Teltowkanal, three West Berlin policeman, drinking Coca Cola, asked, "Would you like one?"

At 3:30 p.m. at Forsthausallee, three women and a man called out to the sentry: "Can you shoot that crow? It's getting on our nerves."

At 10:00 p.m. at Heidekampgraben, a policeman asked: "Hi boys, are the mosquitoes bad over there too?"

At 8:40 a.m. at the Köllnische Heide sentry post, a girl about sixteen years old on the second story of the house at Wegastraße 36 removed her pullover and displayed her breasts. At 9:20 a.m. she put her pullover back on.

At 6:10 p.m. at Puderstraße, watchdog Trux bit through the fencing on the dog track and attacked a commander and his assistant on patrol. Twelve shots were fired and the dog died.

At 10:00 a.m. at Harzer Straße, a driver and a co-worker in a beer delivery van, registration B-CL 51, offered the sentries beer "if you come over."

At 12:59 p.m. at Lohmühlenstraße, a family in number 58/59 waved to a woman on the West Berlin side.

At 3:02 p.m. at Bahnhofstraße, a man in his mid-twenties said: "Go home and make yourself a cup of coffee."

At 3:40 p.m. at Lohmühlenstraße, a woman about twenty years old called out four times: "Come on over, you can have me."

At 7:05 p.m. at Kiefholzstraße, two girls, about fifteen years old, called to the sentry: "We love you! Come on over, we need something."

At 1:30 p.m. at Bethaniendamm, a West Berlin customs official threw an empty lemonade bottle over the wall.

At 11:30 p.m. at Elsenstraße, three young women said: "Come on over, we've got the place to ourselves."

At 4:56 p.m. at Alexandrinenstraße, a man shouted at the sentries: "Have you really thought about it?"

At 3:12 p.m. at Checkpoint Charlie, an American soldier held up a 25 x 30 cm photo of a nude woman.

At 2:03 p.m. at Ackerstraße, a man on a viewing platform threw his hat over the wall.

At 5:13 p.m. at the Marschall Bridge, a female corpse was found in the water barricades.

At 12:20 a.m at Nordgraben, two men shouted to the sentry post: "Say something!"

At 10:15 a.m. at Wolliner Straße, an old lady threw a bag of oranges over the wall.

At 1:13 a.m. at Korsörer Straße, two men threw a pack of cigarettes (brand Ernte 23) over the wall, saying "You can smoke these."

At 5:15 p.m. at Schulzestraße, a sixteen-year-old boy on the S-Bahn rail platform said: "I have a question. What time is it?"

2

Border guard ████████ was commended for preventing a breach of the border with his watchdog Cella.

Border guard ████████████ was commended for keeping his motorcycle in excellent condition.

Border guard ██████████ was commended for his measured and exemplary appearance.

Border guard ████████████ was commended for fulfilling military norms.

Border guard ████████ was commended for advocating the politics of the state in conversations with the other comrades in the barracks.

Border guard ████████ was commended for encouraging his comrades to achieve higher performances.

Border guard █████████████████ was commended for having his weapons locker win first place among all regiment lockers.

Border guard ███████████ was commended for excellent performance as a member of the chemical group.

Border guard ██████████ was commended for his correct actions.

Border guard █████████████ was commended for his class-appropriate manner when faced with enemy provocation at the border.

3

Border guard ████████ was censured for lacking ideological clarity.

Border guard █████████████ was censured for sleeping in the watchtower.

Border guard ███████ was censured for telling a comrade that he would like to go the West for just one day to visit a brothel.

Border guard ███████████ was censured for lackadaisically performing his early morning gymnastics and not bothering to touch his toes.

Border guard █████████████ was censured for copying passages from Franz Kafka in his diary.

Border guard ████████████████ was censured for owning a toy Mercedes automobile with an integrated measuring tape.

Border guard ████████████ was censured for being a committed fan of beat music.

Border guard ███████████ was censured for falling prey to ideological diversion due to his religious convictions.

Border guard ████████ was censured for making shapes in the snow with his feet, out of boredom.

Border guard ██████████ was censured for firing single shots instead of shooting in short bursts.

Border guard █████████ was censured for being afraid.

Border guard █████████████ was censured for shooting his gun at such an angle that the border violator was not forced to stop.

Border guard █████████████ was censured for committing suicide by hanging.

4

January 28, 1969: Eighty shots were fired at possible border violator Manfred ███████ at Kremmener Straße, near the Friedrich-Ludwig-Jahn sports fields. None struck the target, but he was captured, interrogated by the State Security Police and turned over to a People's Police force car unit. He was discovered to be in a state of inebriation.

April 9, 1969: 148 shots from two watch towers were fired at border violator Johannes Lange of Dresden. Fire ceased when the border violator had been destroyed. All of the eight border guards received commendations and three were given a material bonus of a wristwatch.

February 2, 1969: 48 shots were fired at an unknown border violator at the Massante Bridge who was carrying a 3.5-meter wooden plank, which he leaned against the wall and scurried up. His fate is unknown.

November 10, 1965: 17 shots were fired at border violator Heinz Cyrus ██████, a milkman from the island of Rügen. None struck the target. He fled into a building at Gartenstraße 85, ran up the stairs to the roof and attempted to hide by hanging from the gutter. The gutter collapsed, and he fell four stories and died in the People's Police Hospital (Scharnhorststraße) the following day.

November 11, 1969: 34 shots were fired at Heinz-Jürgen ████████, a fourteen-year-old, in the water under the Oberbaum Bridge. Earlier in the day, the boy had been questioned at Police Station 85 about a theft and was scared to go home. None of the shots struck the target, but the boy was apprehended by boat and arrested.

April 29, 1966: 176 shots were fired at Paul Stretz, a West Berliner who, in an advanced state of inebriation, had decided to go for a swim in the Spandau Shipping Canal, in East Berlin territory. Mistaken for a border violator, four of the shots struck the target, who was destroyed.

August 18, 1964: One fatal shot was fired by border guard ██████ ██████, age twenty, in the back of possible border violator Hildegard Trabant, age thirty-seven, of Tilsiter Straße. She was discovered hiding behind an elder bush beside abandoned railroad tracks at Schönhauser Allee, sixty meters from the border. Her personal effects, returned to her husband, a member of the People's Police force, were:

an identity card
Party card, membership No. 146,664
144.28 East German marks
1 key chain with keys
5 handkerchiefs
1 pair of shoes
1 blue slip
1 pair of stockings
1 dress suit
1 bottle of perfume
1 pair of sunglasses
1 pair of eyeglasses
1 nail clippers
1 comb
12 cigarettes (Jubilar brand)
1 pen
1 notebook
1 postcard, sent September 12, 1963, from a relative in Recklinghausen
1 package of tampons (Neo brand)

Once upon a Time in Albania

MARRIAGE

A young man takes no part in the arrangement of his marriage.

A young woman takes no part in the arrangement of her marriage.

A young man may reject his intended.

If a young woman, with her father's consent, rejects her intended, she may not marry until her intended dies, even if he takes another wife.

If a young woman, without her father's consent, rejects her intended, she is forcibly handed over, and a bullet is given by the father to the young man. If she attempts to flee, the young man may kill her with the bullet. No blood feud ensues.

On the day of the marriage, the bridegroom's men fetch the bride. Each of the bridegroom's men must come to the wedding with a sheep. If the bride has died, they carry her corpse back to the bridegroom's house.

FAMILY

The husband corrects the wife, and may beat or bind her when his words are scorned.

The wife who commits adultery is shot in the back. No blood feud ensues.

The father buys weapons for his sons when they come of age. Daughters are provided with clothing and shoes until they marry.

The father may beat or bind his children. If he kills his child, it is considered that the child has committed suicide.

Children of any age remain obedient to the father until he dies and must seek his approval for all things.

If a man has no sons, his daughter may inherit his property if she chooses to dress and act like a man. She may not marry.

OATHS

An oath is a denial of guilt.

Women and children cannot swear an oath.

An oath cannot merely be spoken: He who swears an oath must be touching a cross, a rock, or the heads of his sons.

Once an oath is sworn, the man is considered innocent and the charge is dropped.

If an oath is falsely sworn, a man incurs divine punishment and his family is dishonored for seven generations. One hundred sheep and one ox must be paid.

HONOR

God has touched our foreheads with two fingers of honor. All men are equal. The handsome and the ugly are the same.

A man is dishonored if he is called a liar in front of other men; if someone spits at him or pushes him or threatens him; if his wife is insulted or if his wife runs off with another man; if someone takes his weapons off his shoulder or belt; if someone insults his friend; if someone removes the lid of a cooking pot in his hearth; if someone in his house dips a morsel of food before the guest does, dishonoring both him and his guest.

There is no fine for an offense to honor, nor can it be paid for in property. An offense to honor can never be forgiven. An offense to honor can only be paid with blood.

A guest is welcomed. His weapons are hung on a hook. More logs
are brought; the guest stirs the fire. His feet are washed. Coffee
is taken first by the guest and then the master of the house. Raki,
however, is taken first by the master of the house and then by the
guest. A high-ranking guest is given the sheep's head, which he
smashes with his fist. A lower-ranking guest is given the shoulder
of the sheep; he strips the meat and cracks the bone to extract
the marrow. The guest must be the first to stop eating and to stop
drinking raki.

TRADE

Prices are regulated for an iron cauldron, a copper still, a good pan
for baking bread, an oak tree for timber, unwashed wool, beaten
wool felt, mohair, a hive with bees, honey, wax, wine, grape raki,
cheese, unmelted butter, melted butter, dried pork, coffee, a pair
of thin sandals, a pair of thick sandals, all farm animals, a rifle, and
a pistol inlaid with silver coins.

A murder is paid for in blood. Or it may be paid by livestock, land,
or guns.

Note: The codification of the *Kanun*, the customary laws of the northern Albanian
mountains, is traditionally attributed to Lekë Dukagjini (1410–1481). The laws themselves are many centuries older, possibly dating to the Bronze Age Illyrians, and were
modified after the time of Lekë, to account for such things as modern weaponry.

Bush the Postmodernist

In the late 1960s, George Bush Jr. was at Yale, branding the buttocks of pledges to the Delta Kappa Epsilon fraternity with a hot coat hangar. Michel Foucault was at the Société Française de Philosophie, considering the question, "What is an author?"

The two, needless to say, never met. Foucault may have visited Texas on one of his lecture tours, but Junior, as far as it is known, never took his S&M revelry beyond the Ivy League—novelists will have to invent a chance encounter in a basement club in Austin. Moreover, Junior's general ignorance of all things, except for professional sports, naturally extended to the nation known as France. On his first trip to Paris in 2002, Junior, now President of the United States, stood beside Jacques Chirac at a press conference and said, "He's always saying that the food here is fantastic and I'm going to give him a chance to show me tonight."

Foucault found his theories embodied, sometimes unconvincingly, in writers such as Proust or Flaubert. He died in 1984, while Junior was still an aging frat boy, and didn't live to see this far more applicable text. For the questions that he, even then, declared hopelessly obsolete are the very ones that should not be asked about *Decision Points* "by" George W. Bush (or by "George W. Bush"):

> Who really spoke? Is it really he and not someone else? With what authenticity or originality? And what part of his deepest self did he express in his discourse?

Decision Points holds the same relation to George W. Bush as a line of fashion accessories or a perfume does to the movie star that bears its name; he no doubt served in some advisory capacity. The words themselves have been assembled by Chris Michel (the young speechwriter and devoted acolyte who went to Yale with Bush's daughter

Barbara); a freelance editor, Sean Desmond; the staff at Crown Publishers (who reportedly paid $7 million for the book); a team of a dozen researchers; and scores of "trusted friends." Foucault: "What difference does it make who is speaking?" "The mark of the writer is ... nothing more than the singularity of his absence."

As a postmodern text, many passages in the book are pastiches of moments from other books, including scenes that Bush himself did not witness. These are taken from the memoirs of members of the Bush administration and journalistic accounts such as Bob Woodward's *Plan for Attack* and *Bush at War*. To complete the cycle of postmodernity, there are bits of dialogue lifted from Woodward, who is notorious for inventing dialogue.

Occasionally, someone on Team *DP* will insert a lyrical phrase—the tears on the begrimed faces of the 9/11 relief workers "cutting a path through the soot like rivulets through a desert"—but most of the prose sounds like this:

> I told Margaret and Deputy Chief of Staff Josh Bolten that I considered this a far-reaching decision. I laid out a process for making it. I would clarify my guiding principles, listen to experts on all sides of the debate, reach a tentative conclusion, and run it past knowledgeable people. After finalizing a decision, I would explain it to the American people. Finally, I would set up a process to ensure that my policy was implemented.

There are nearly 500 pages of this, reminiscent of the current po-mo poster boys, Tao Lin, with his anaesthicized declarative sentences, and Kenneth Goldsmith with his "noncreative writing," such as a transcription of a year's worth of daily radio weather reports. Foucault notes: "Today's writing has freed itself from the theme of expression."

Even the title of the book unchains the signifier from the signified. "Decision points" is business-speak for a list of factors, usually marked by a bullet in Powerpoint presentations, that should be considered before making a decision. There are no decision points in

Decision Points. Despite what is claimed above, Bush never stops to consider. He is the Decider who acts impulsively and "crisply," drawing on his "moral clarity." (In the scariest line in the book, he has allowed to let slip that his motive for the invasions of Afghanistan and Iraq was simple revenge, surely the least desirable emotional quality one would want in a world leader with access to nuclear weapons. About 9/11 the text says: "My blood was boiling. We were going to find out who did this, and kick their ass.")

Team *DP* has indeed "creat[ed] a space into which the writing subject constantly disappears"; one learns almost nothing about George W. Bush from this book. The names of hundreds of other people are mentioned, almost always in praise—it is, in its way, the world's longest prize acceptance speech—but none of them, outside of the Bush family, have any life as a character. Each new person is introduced with a single sentence, noting one or more of the following: 1) Texan origins; 2) college athletic achievements; 3) military service; 4) deep religious faith. The sentence ends with three personal characteristics: "honest, ethical, and forthright"; "a brilliant mind, disarming modesty, and a buoyant spirit"; "a statesman, a savvy lawyer, and a magnet for talented people"; "smart, thoughtful, energetic" (that's Condi); "knowledgeable, articulate, and confident" (that's Rummy); "a wise, principled, humane man" (Clarence Thomas); and so on. Then the person does whatever Bush tells him to do.

Bush is the lone hero of every page of *Decision Points*. Very few spoken words are assigned to him, outside of the public records of speeches and press conferences, and in nearly all of them he is forceful, in command, and peeved at the inadequacies of his subordinates:

> "What the hell is happening?" I asked during an NSC meeting in late April. "Why isn't anybody stopping these looters?"

> "By the time Colin gets to the White House for the meeting, this had better be fixed."

"We need to find out what he knows," I directed the team. "What are our options?"

"Damn right," I said.

"Where the hell is Ashcroft?" I asked.

"Go," I said. "This is the right thing to do."

"We're going to stay confident and patient, cool and steady," I said.

"Damn it, we can do more than one thing at a time," I told the national security team.

As I told my advisers, "I didn't take this job to play small ball."

"This is a good start, but it's not enough," I told him. "Go back to the drawing board and think even bigger."

"We don't have twenty-four hours," I snapped. "We've waited too long already."

"What the hell is going on?" I asked Hank. "I thought we were going to get a deal."

"That's it?" I snapped.

As Foucault says: "The author's name serves to characterize a certain mode of being of discourse."

This is a chronicle of the Bush Era with no colored-coded Terror Alerts; no Freedom Fries; no Halliburton; no Healthy Forest Initiative (which opened up wilderness areas to logging); no Clear Skies

Act (which reduced air pollution standards); no New Freedom Initiative (which proposed testing all Americans, beginning with school children, for mental illness); no pamphlets sold by the National Parks Service explaining that the Grand Canyon was created by the Flood; no research by the National Institutes of Health on whether prayer can cure cancer ("imperative," because poor people have limited access to health care); no cover-up of the death of football star Pat Tillman by "friendly fire" in Afghanistan; no "Total Information Awareness" from the Information Awareness Office; no Project for the New American Century; no invented heroic rescue of Pvt. Jessica Lynch; no Fox News; no hundreds of millions spent on "abstinence education." It does not deal with the Cheney theory of the "unitary executive"—essentially that neither the Congress nor the courts can tell the president what to do—or Bush's frequent use of "signing statements" to indicate that he would completely ignore a bill that the Congress had just passed.

It is astonishing how many major players from Bush World are here Missing in Action. Entirely absent, or mentioned only once in passing, are Paul Wolfowitz, Richard Perle, John Yoo, Elliott Abrams, Ahmed Chalabi, Ayad Allawi, Rick Santorum, Trent Lott, Tom DeLay, Richard Armitage, Katherine Harris, Ken Mehlman, Paul O'Neill, Rush Limbaugh. Barely appearing at all are John Ashcroft, Samuel Alito, Ari Fleischer, Alberto Gonzalez, Denny Hastert, John Negroponte, and Tom Ridge. Condi and Colin Powell are given small parts, but Rummy is largely a passing shadow. No one is allowed to steal a scene from the star.

The enormous black hole in the book is the Grand Puppetmaster himself, Dick Cheney, the man who was prime minister to Bush's figurehead president. In *Decision Points*, as in the Bush years, he is nearly always hiding in an undisclosed location. When he does show up on scattered pages, he is merely another member of the Bush team. The implicit message is that Washington was too small a town for two Deciders.

Only twice in this fat book does one get a sense of Cheney's presence. He complains about Bush's refusal to grant a pardon to Scooter Libby: "I can't believe you're going to leave a soldier on the battlefield." (But the scene is taken from a news article, where the line is not attributed to Cheney but to an anonymous staffer, and spoken about Bush, not directly to him.) And there is one glimpse at how adept Cheney was at pushing Bush's macho buttons:

> Dick Cheney was concerned about the slow diplomatic process. He warned that Saddam Hussein could be using the time to produce weapons, hide weapons, or plot an attack. At one of our weekly lunches that winter, Dick asked me directly, "Are you going to take care of this guy, or not?" That was his way of saying he thought we had given diplomacy enough time. I appreciated Dick's blunt advice. I told him I wasn't ready to move yet. "Okay, Mr. President, it's your call," he said. Then he deployed one of his favorite lines. "That's why they pay you the big bucks," he said with a gentle smile.

If Cheney has been left on the cutting room floor, the surprise supporting actor is Dad. We all know too much about the Bush Family Drama: Dad the Phi Beta Kappa student and star collegiate athlete, Junior at the same schools a mediocre goofball who could never make the team and was reduced to being a cheerleader; Dad the World War II fighter pilot hero (actually considered a coward outside of Kennebunkport, but that's another story), Junior mainly AWOL from the dinky Texas Air National Guard; Dad the successful oil man, Junior losing fortunes on dry wells, continually bailed out by Dad's friends. When the black sheep loser—and not his reliable brother Jeb, who was groomed for the task—bizarrely became president, Junior made a point of selecting two unilateral *Pax Americana* hotheads, Cheney and Rumsfeld, whom diplomatic Dad couldn't stand. His obsession with taking out Saddam—which, contrary to *Decision Points*, was evident on Day One of the administration—was widely seen as a reaction to Dad's "failure" (according to the Project for the New American Century crowd) to invade Baghdad during the Gulf War. Even Dad's best friend, Brent Scowcroft, came out publicly against the imminent war. During the presidency, Junior was touchy on the subject, and famously replied, when asked if he sought his father's advice, "I appeal to a higher father."

Unexpectedly, Dad is everywhere in the book, with father and son continually declaring their mutual pride and undying love. Team *DP* even feels the need to quote in their entirety Dad's words when Junior is elected president for the second (well, actually the first) time: "Congratulations, son." The configuration of piety, patriotism, filial justification, and self-aggrandizement is in this, perhaps the most typical dramatic passage in the book:

> I was standing next to Mother and Dad at a Christmas Eve car-oling session when the Navy chaplain walked over. He said, "Sir, I've just returned from Wilford Hall in San Antonio, where the wounded troops lie. I told the boys that if they had a message for the president, I'd be seeing you tonight."
>
> He continued: "They said, 'Please tell the president we're proud to serve a great country, and we're proud to serve a great man like George Bush.'" Dad's eyes filled with tears.

(It may well be that Navy chaplains employ such locutions as "where the wounded troops lie," but in any event, there are quite a few scenes of grown men weeping in *Decision Points*, most of them in uniform and listening to Bush speak. The book, perhaps deliberately playing to its intended audience, is very much like country & western music: one minute they're raising hell and the next they're jerking tears.)

Mother—she's never Mom—pops up frequently with a withering remark. As middle-aged Junior runs a marathon, Mother and Dad are, of course, coming out of church. Standing on the steps, Dad cheers "That's my boy!" and Mother shouts "Keep moving, George! There are some fat people ahead of you!" When Junior decides to run for governor, Mother's reaction is simply: "George, you can't win." Not cited is Mother's indelible comment on the Iraq War: "Why should we hear about body bags and deaths? Why should I waste my beautiful mind on something like that?" But the single newsworthy item in this entire book is the get-this-boy-to-therapy scene where Mother has a miscarriage at home, asks teenaged Junior to drive her to the hospital, and shows him the fetus of his sibling, which for some reason she has put in a jar.

Bush claims this was the moment when he became "pro-life," unalterably opposed to abortion and, later, embryonic stem-cell research. (The thought would not have occurred to Mother. At the time, patrician Republicans like the Bushes were birth-control advocates; like Margaret Sanger, they didn't want the unwashed masses wildly reproducing. Dad was even on the board of the Texas branch of Planned Parenthood.)

Decision Points flaunts its postmodernity by blurring the distinction between fiction and non-fiction. That is to say, the parts that are not outright lies—particularly the accounts of Hurricane Katrina and the lead-up to the Iraq War—are the sunnier halves of half-truths. The legions of amateur investigative journalists on the internet—as usual, doing the job the major media no longer performs—are busily compiling lists of those lies. Gerhard Schroeder has already stated that the passage in which he appears is completely false. And even Mother has weighed in. Interviewed recently on television, she said she never showed Junior that jar, but maybe "Paula" did. (It was assumed we would know that Paula was the maid.)

More generally, the *DP* Bush bears little relation to the George W. Bush of memory. The *DPB* is always poring over reports; GWB insisted on one-paragraph summaries, usually delivered orally. (Rumsfeld, who knew his man, presented his daily reports with shiny color covers that had a stirring combat photo accompanied by an inspirational line from the Bible.) The *DPB* continually mentions his favorite books and maintains that he read two a week while president; GWB was rumored to be dyslexic, and read no book other than the Book (much like his counterpart, that other wealthy bad boy, Osama bin Laden). GWB famously never asked anything at meetings, but the *DPB* claims:

> I learn best by asking questions. In some cases, I probe to understand a complex issue. Other times, I deploy questions as a way to test my briefers' knowledge. If they cannot answer concisely and in plain English, it raises a red flag that they may not fully grasp the subject.

The *DPB* works tirelessly to keep the free world free; GWB spent long hours in the White House gym and took more vacations than any other president. The twenty-nine-year-old *DPB* goes to Beijing to visit Dad, then Ambassador, thinks about the French and Russian revolutions, and learns important lessons about liberty and justice; the real GWB said at the time that he went to "date Chinese women."

In the book, as in his life, Bush the postmodernist is a simulacrum: a Connecticut blueblood who pretended to be a Texas cowboy, though he couldn't ride a horse and lived on a "ranch" with no cattle. He was, and is, happiest when surrounded by professionals in the three areas in which he was a notable failure: athletics, the military, and business. He is like a sports fan who dresses up in the team jersey to watch the game. References to his "military service" recur frequently throughout the book, as though it were actually more than a few months spent avoiding it. He was the only modern American president to appear in public in a military uniform—even Eisenhower never wore his while president—like a ribboned despot from a banana republic. He has said that one of his proudest moments was throwing out the ceremonial first pitch in a World Series game. The frontispiece to the book is the photo of Bush in his other proud moment, standing in the ruins of the Twin Towers with his cheerleader bullhorn, just one of the relief worker guys.

A pup in a kennel of alpha males, inadequate compared to Dad, humiliated by Mother, he classically became a bully to compensate:

an ass-brander, noted for what he calls verbal "needling"; a boss who cussed out his subordinates and invented demeaning nicknames for everyone around him; a president who taunted terrorists, most of them imaginary, and challenged them to "bring it on."

He was notoriously oblivious to suffering, including the torture of alleged terrorists, which he openly and unequivocally approved. Who can forget his mocking, while governor, of Karla Faye Tucker, whom even the Pope tried to save from the electric chair? Or his humorous "who's hiding the WMDs?" performance at the White House Correspondents dinner? Or that Bush, the military man, cut benefits for veterans and did nothing about appalling conditions in veterans' hospitals? Or that he decimated the agencies that protect public health and safety?

The book states that, for him, the worst moment of his presidency was—not 9/11, or the hundreds of thousands he killed or maimed, or the millions he made homeless in Iraq and jobless in the United States—but when the rapper Kanye West said, in a fundraiser for Katrina victims, that Bush didn't care about black people.

West was only half right. Bush is not particularly racist. He never portrayed Hispanics as hordes of scary invaders; Condi was his workout buddy and virtually his second wife; he was in awe of Colin Powell; and he was most comfortable in the two most integrated sectors of American society, the military and professional sports. It wasn't that he didn't care about black people. Outside of his family, he didn't care about people, and Billy Graham taught him that "we cannot earn God's love through good deeds"—only through His grace, which Bush knew he had already received.

As of this writing, *Decision Points* has sold almost a million and a half copies. Conservative groups buy these things in bulk, and it was the perfect Christmas gift for one's Republican uncle. Moreover, in the mere two years since he left Washington, Bush is beginning to seem like a reasonable man, compared to the Republicans who have now been elected to higher office. Unlike them, he is not a "family values" Christian who likes to have prostitutes dress him in diapers; he does not advocate burning the Quran; he does not believe that Obama is a Kenyan Muslim allied with terrorists who is building internment camps for dissidents; he does not believe that people of Hispanic origin should be randomly stopped and asked to prove their immigration status; he does not support a military invasion of Mexico or a constitutional amendment stating that the United States cannot be subject to Sharia law or an electric fence along the entire Canadian border or the death penalty for doctors who provide abortions; he does not believe that bicycle lanes in major cities are part of a plot by the United Nations to impose a single world government. Bush is no Tea Partier; he and Cheney and Fox News merely unleashed them, as Mao did for the Red Guards.

Despite the sales, it's unlikely that many will ever read *Decision Points*, and even fewer will finish it. Those who do will find three revelations, besides the fetus in the jar. Junior killed his sister Doro's goldfish by pouring vodka in the fishbowl. He was convinced he should run for president after hearing a sermon about Moses leading the Israelites out of Egypt. And, as a man who likes to go to bed early, at 10 p.m. on the night of September 11, 2001, President George W. Bush was complaining that he needed to get to sleep.

He believes that this book will "prove useful as you make choices in your own life."

[NOVEMBER 2010]

118

Khubilai Khan at the Met

1

The Mongols inhabited a vast, featureless grass plain where the soil was too thin for crops. They raised horses, cattle, yaks, sheep, and goats, and subsisted almost entirely on meat and milk and milk products. The women milked the cows and the men milked the mares. They had no fixed houses and lived in yurts made of greased felt that they hauled on ox-drawn carts. Inside the yurts, hunks of meat hung on the horns of goats. They never washed their clothes or washed their vessels; bathing in running water was punishable by death. The women were excellent equestrians and archers, but female corpulence was prized and the wealthiest among them became too obese to ride. They had no written language and only rudimentary skills in metallurgy; unlike the Crusaders, they never made horseshoes. Their human genius was in military organization and tactics, and in politics as war by other means.

Nomads continually need greater territory for fresh pasture, and the peoples of the grasslands—Mongol, Tatar, Merkit, Uriyankat, Oirat, Tumet, Kerait, Naiman, Ongut—had been at war for centuries. As early as the 3rd century BCE, the settled and agricultural Chinese had begun construction of the Great Wall to keep them out. This was only sporadically successful: By the 13th century, the Tanguts in the northwest had already founded the Xi Xia Dynasty, and most of the rest of northern China was under control of the Jurchens, who had established the Jin Dynasty after conquering, in turn, the Liao Dynasty, ruled by another northern tribe, the Khitan.

In 1206, a Mongol of obscure birth, Temüjin, after much internecine warfare, united the tribes of the steppes and was declared the Chinggis (Genghis) Khan, the "universal ruler." Within a few decades, he and his successors controlled an empire that stretched from Korea to Poland. They destroyed dynasties that had governed for centuries and some of the most cosmopolitan and sophisticated cities on earth. Samarkand and Bukhara never recovered their glory; in the Silk Road city of Merv, perhaps the largest in the world, a million and a half were killed; in Balakh, it was said that only a few dogs were left barking in the empty streets. Moscow and Kiev fell, Isfahan and Damascus; 800,000 were killed in Baghdad; a million in Chengdu; in Aleppo only the craftsmen were spared; in Poland they cut off one ear of every surviving male and collected them in bags. It was merely the fortuitous deaths of Chinggis's successors that kept the Mongols out of Egypt and Europe all the way to the Atlantic.

The Mongols overran one-fifth of the earth with forces inferior in number, but unmatched in military tactics and political skill. Among warring kingdoms, they would join with one side to defeat the other, and then destroy their ally. Unlike the Arab nomads who had conquered in the name of Islam, or the European Crusaders who fought for Christ, the Mongols had no ideology. They founded no civilization, only devastated cultures or let them be. After Chinggis vanquished the Xi Xia and Jin dynasties, he planned to kill all the people and turn the entirety of northern China into pasture land for his horses. He was persuaded that it would be more lucrative to allow the Chinese to continue their livelihoods and simply tax them.

Khans succeeded to the throne by tanistry—elected by a convocation of chieftains—not inheritance, though the khans had so many children with their wives and concubines that successors were normally blood relatives who had defeated or killed their brothers or cousins. By 1260, when Chinggis's grandson Khubilai was declared the Great Khan, the empire was already divided into four vast tracts under semi-autonomous command. Khubilai nominally ruled them all, but he directly controlled the eastern and richest sector: northern China, Korea, Tibet, and Mongolia itself.

Khubilai was a warrior shepherd ruling the most advanced civilization on earth at the time. In his kingdom there were a few hundred thousand Mongols, most of them in Mongolia itself, and some ten million Chinese who unsurprisingly did not welcome yet another foreign occupation. The genius of his success was that he simultaneously weakened the power of the Chinese while increasing his popularity by making himself seemingly more Chinese, although he couldn't read and could barely speak the language.

He moved the capital of the empire south and east from Khara Khorum in Mongolia, first to Shangdu (the Xanadu of Marco Polo and Coleridge, now survived by only a few stones and broken statues) and then to the former Jin Dynasty capital of Zhongdu (the Central Capital, present-day Beijing). He renamed it Dadu (the Great Capital) and built a magnificent city in the Chinese style with the tens of thousands of artisans who had been forcibly relocated from various corners of the Khanate. He lived like a Chinese emperor, though he preferred to sleep in a yurt on the palace grounds, and in 1271 proclaimed a new dynasty, the Yuan.

Yuan meant "origin"—as in "back to the origins"—and Khubilai revived ancient Confucian court rituals and had a dynastic history written in the traditional manner to justify its heaven-endowed legitimacy. His greatest claim as a Chinese emperor was that the Yuan eventually unified the country as it had not been in centuries. The Jin had conquered half of the Song Dynasty, but the southern portion continued on for 150 years. The Southern Song, a wealthier and more populated region, with some fifty million people, had become weak and bankrupt as—in a scenario that has become all too familiar—the rich managed to legally avoid paying taxes while military expenses greatly increased. Nevertheless, it took years for Khubilai to conquer them and he never overcame their resentment, for the southerners were unaccustomed to foreign occupation and Confucian wisdom dictated that one must remain loyal to one's original master. The rich, however, were allowed to keep their lands and were not unhappy to become even richer with the prospering sea and land trade.

To lessen the political power of the oceanic Chinese majority, Khubilai abolished the examination system, which traditionally had been the only way to rise into and through the bureaucracy. The exams were based on a knowledge of the Confucian classics and it was unlikely that non-Chinese would be able to pass; appointments were now made under the Mongol system of personal recommendations. A four-tier system was created. At the top were, of course, Mongols, who were more or less forced to keep their identity. They were forbidden to marry Chinese, or even to speak the language. Official proceedings were done through interpreters, though Khubilai unsuccessfully attempted to introduce a new, alphabetic form of writing, devised by a Tibetan monk, that could represent the sounds of all the languages of the empire.

Next in the hierarchy were the "colored-eyed people," the foreigners, largely from western Asia. One could now travel safely by land from the eastern Mediterranean to the China Sea, and merchants poured in, welcome as long as they exchanged their gold and silver for Khubilai's paper currency. Many of them—including Marco Polo, if he is to be believed—were given government positions.

Third were the northern Chinese, and fourth, the least trustworthy of all, the southern Chinese. Power in that other political force— organized religion—was kept in check by promoting all of them and favoring none. Along with adherents of the traditional Three Teachings (Confucianism, Taoism, Buddhism) there were Nestorian Christians, Manicheans, and Muslims. Among the Buddhists, preference was shown for the Tibetan version, which was more appealing to Khubilai with its magical powers and politically motivated lamas, than the more contemplative Chinese schools of Chan (which became in Zen in Japan). There were, however, instances of religious repression: periodically against the Muslims, who were over-enthusiastic collectors of taxes, and once against the Taoists, when Khubilai sided with the Buddhists in a dispute and ordered Taoist temples to be evacuated and the books of their canon burned.

Whether Khubilai was crueler than previous Chinese emperors is subject to debate. He created the most comprehensive surveillance system of his citizens, unmatched until the time of Mao, but he executed fewer officials. In the wars he fought, he was responsible for the deaths of hundreds of thousands, perhaps millions, including his disastrous campaigns against Annam and Champa (in present-day Vietnam), where his horses could not survive the jungle, the Kingdom of Java, and Japan, where nine hundred ships with the corpses of naked Japanese women nailed to the sides were destroyed by a combination of samurais and the *kamikaze* (divine wind) of a typhoon, whose symbolism would resurface in Japanese propaganda in World War II.

His later years were an autumn of the patriarch. He lost his favorite wife and favorite son, became grotesquely fat, suffering from gout and other ailments, and detached from governing. He held huge and endless banquets of meat and koumiss, fermented mare's milk, and was in a near-continual state of inebriation. More and more time was spent in the summer palace of Shangdu, which was largely a hunting reserve. There, four elephants would carry him, lying on a couch, in a gold-plated palanquin decked with tiger skins, accompanied by five hundred falconers and leopards and lynxes trained to chase down bears and wild boars.

He died in 1294 and was succeeded by twelve khans in turn, including ten in one seventeen-year span. China was wracked with natural disasters: unusual cold in what is now known as the Little Ice Age, famines every two years, floods, swarms of locusts, the earthquake of 1303 that killed at least a half a million, and epidemics of typhoid, smallpox, and bubonic plague. (It was the Mongols who brought the Black Death to Europe in the 14th century, which some epidemiologists trace back to the fleas on the Mongolian gerbils of the steppes.) It is probable that the total population dropped by tens of millions. In the Chinese obsession with the harmony of Heaven and Earth, with the emperor as the Son of Heaven who assures order, it meant that the universe was out of whack, that there was a moral disorder as much as a physical one. In 1368 the dynasty collapsed in the usual chaos and a new dynasty, the Ming, was declared.

2

The great museums are little empires, ruled by tyrannical or benevolent emperors, with the plunder of the world arranged geographically: the Great Powers of history centrally located and the more remote corners of the earth usually accessible only through a labyrinth of corridors, stairs, and elevators. Small wonder, then, that museums so often pitch their blockbuster shows on empires themselves and, when possible, charismatic emperors.

"The World of Khubilai Khan" at the Metropolitan Museum is no exception. Khubilai—thanks to Marco Polo, Coleridge, and a thousand cheesy discos called Xanadu—is a brand name of sorts. It hardly matters that Marco Polo may never have gone to China and that Coleridge's opium dream—beyond the "stately pleasure dome" of the first lines—was also an amalgam of his readings of actual and fantastic accounts of travel in Florida, Kashmir, and on the Nile. Blockbusters have to sell tickets, and the Met is even luring visitors with a Patti Smith "tribute to Xanadu" concert. The exhibition itself is a majestic array of paintings, sculpture, calligraphy, ceramics, textiles, and assorted knicknacks, gathered from many museum collections and beautifully and dramatically presented. So perhaps it is pedantic to note that little of this has anything to do with Khubilai Khan. Most of the works were created before or after his reign, often in lands that were not then under his control. Nor is the subtitle of the show, "Chinese Art in the Yuan Dynasty" exactly accurate, as there are many works from the Jin, Xi Xia, and Southern Song. To put it another way, according to Met typology, we are still living in the World of Franklin Roosevelt, a world that began about the time of the Civil War and includes the artworks of Mexican muralists and Haitian folk painters.

The received wisdom on the Yuan Dynasty has been that, however wealthy from trade, it was a semi-barbaric time, vastly inferior to the refined accomplishments of the Song. Artisans were prized over artists, the tradition of court patronage of the arts and educating emperors in connoisseurship was largely ended, and the intellectual class was attenuated with the end of the examination system. The Met has gone to the other extreme, claiming that "artistically the Yuan was one of the most brilliant periods in Chinese history." Certainly the exhibition has gathered magnificent pieces in the attempt to demonstrate this. But the catalog essays, which often digress into discussions of other periods and largely ignore the considerable bad news of the time, never quite manage to say that, unlike other empires, there were few direct connections between the Mongols and the art created under their rule. Much of Yuan art was stylistically a continuation of what had happened before, and it was produced in spite of, oblivious to, or even in active opposition to the khans.

Confucianism taught that when the government is bad, one should head for the hills. (Taoism taught that, regardless of government, one should head for the hills.) After the fall of the Southern Song, many of the best southern painters went into reclusion in the area of Lake Tai, while many northern intellectuals, taking advantage of the unification, went south. Rather than wall hangings, which are a public art, they turned to painting scrolls—which are meant to be examined privately—of Taoist landscapes, with or without tiny figures admiring the scene. One of the exceptions was Zhao Mengfu, who actually served Khubilai, reforming the currency and postal systems. Considered a traitor by his friends, Zhao claimed he was following a kind of "reclusion at court," serving the government while maintaining detachment. The work shown at the Met—and he was indeed a great painter—represents both sides: beautiful Taoist landscapes and what must be considered "official" portraits of horses.

The horse is a complicated symbol in the Yuan, not only associated with the Mongol horsemen of the steppes, but also with the horse-obsessed Tang Dynasty. Thus the portrayal of a healthy horse meant not only that the present government was benevolent, but that it was a continuation of China's golden age. In the exhibition, there is a scroll by Zhao of a determined young man in the red robe of an

125

official, riding toward the capital on a spirited steed, and one of a groom standing next to a horse that is almost ridiculously plump, like a candied apple on four sticks.

Zhao is answered by Gong Kai, a painter who stayed in the south in reclusion, with an astonishing ink drawing of a terribly emaciated horse. The drawing is accompanied by an obliquely pointed inscription:

> Ever since the clouds and mist fell upon the Heavenly Pass,
> The twelve imperial stables of the previous dynasty have been
> empty.
> Who today laments over the bones of this noble steed? [. . .]
>
> One of the classics says that a horse's ribs should be slender and numerous. An ordinary horse has only ten ribs. One with more than this is a noble steed. But only a thousand-league horse has as many as fifteen ribs. If you want to paint the bones beneath the flesh, especially if you intend to make fifteen ribs visible, they will only be visible if the horse is emaciated. With this in mind, I have made this image in order to show that the extraordinary deterioration of this thousand-league horse is not something to be concealed.

The equestrian dialogue is continued by Ren Renfa. He served the government in water management and his "Nine Horses" shows happy animals well-tended by their grooms, an image of official harmony. But his "Two Horses" sends a different message. A robust specimen with a beautiful dappled coat is followed by one that is dull, thin, and feeble, its head cast down. An inscription states that although the second is "an outcast, he doesn't have the burden of galloping all day for his evening feed." Ren then adds a Confucian layer—perhaps to cover his tracks—contrasting the virtuous official who keeps himself lean but fattens the nation and the corrupt official who fattens himself but emaciates the masses. He concludes:

So if you judge a horse only by its external appearance, you really will come to feel ashamed. Therefore, I have inscribed the end of this scroll to await those who will understand it.

The free trade across Asia and the multiculturalism of the empire had little overt effect on Chinese art; artistic influence mainly moved west, where Chinese forms and techniques were transformative in Persian art. One exception was the importation of cobalt, which led to the blue and white porcelains, best known from the subsequent Ming Dynasty and most associated with Chinese ceramics. These were extremely popular in Persia: the Quran forbade eating on gold plates, so the expensive porcelains were a way to exhibit one's wealth at banquets. Moreover, as the Mongols were more interested in commerce than aesthetics, the ceramicists were freed from the design strictures of the Song. Whatever sold worked, and the Yuan is considered a period of experimentation in the decorative arts.

Wonders and curiosities fill the exhibition: The only surviving Mongol hat (Khubilai's wife Chabi invented the idea of a brim for it) and the only surviving glass cup and saucer, in an ethereal blue. Jade belt buckles in a favorite Mongol motif: a falcon attacking a goose. An enormous, mind-boggling Tibetan silk mandala, with Khubilai's great-grandsons, the Emperor Wenzong and his brother, along with their wives, portrayed at the bottom corners as patrons—one of the few instances where there is a direct line between the Mongols and the art of their time. A smiling stone horse floating on clouds. A transcendent hanging scroll of the Bodhisattva Avalokkiteshvara in Water-Moon Manifestation. And the religious mashup of Jesus Christ as a Manichean prophet, sitting cross-legged, like Tibetan images of the Buddha, on a lotus supported by a tiered hexagonal pedestal.

The Yuan was a bad time for poetry, particularly in contrast with the Song. The dominant mode was a kind of proto-rap: lyrics written in slang, where the poet bragged of his sexual prowess, drunkenness, and general bad-boy behavior. The major literary form was the populist play—some 900 were produced—with elaborate costumes and outlandish makeup, where love stories, murder mysteries, and action dramas were periodically interrupted with songs, much like a Bollywood movie. (These would later evolve into the more refined Beijing opera.) In the exhibition are various tiles and sculptures of actors—though from the Jin, not the Yuan—that have been excavated from tombs; presumably the actors were there to amuse the dead in the hereafter.

Most spectacular of all is a hollow porcelain pillow, seven inches high, with an astonishingly detailed scene inside of a play about the Taoist Eight Immortals, set on a stage with intricately formed beaded curtains, a staircase, and latticed windows. Was one meant to dream this particular play, or was it a reminder that dreams themselves are little plays? The pillow takes the French Surrealists one step further: their "theater of dreams" becomes itself a dream. And it serves to remind us that this exhibition of marvels is only named for Khubilai Khan because, five centuries later, an English poet was abruptly awoken.

That Impostor Known as the Buddha

In 125 CE, Aristides, defending Christianity before the Emperor Hadrian at the celebration of the Eleusinian Mysteries, divided the world in four: Greeks (which included Egyptians and Chaldeans), Jews, Christians, and barbarians. The coming of Islam would, in the Christian West, revise this list into a taxonomy that would remain in place for a millennium: Jews, Christians, "Mahometans," and "idolaters." Idolatry eventually included everyone in the non-white world from Aztecs to Taoists, even, during the Crusades, the Mahometans, regardless of their strict prohibitions against graphic representations of God or the Prophet. (In *The Song of Roland* they are seen praying to a menagerie of idols, including Apollo and Lucifer.) Exempt from the charge of idolatry were, of course, the Christians themselves. Their Disneylands of architectural extravaganzas might be filled with colorful and thrilling, terrifying or sentimental images of Jesus and Mary and the saints, but these were not, they explained, objects of worship: They only served as illustrative didactic tools for the illiterate. Not idols for whom prayers were uttered and candles lit, they were edifying comic books.

When those who venerated the image of a grotesquely tortured man arrived in South and East Asia, they were faced with having to account for the apparent sacrality of the image of a man sitting cross-legged on a lotus, with eyes closed and a half-smile on his lips. They had little idea who or what he was, but it was plain that he was an "apparition from a hell," an "impostor," a "monster." Leibniz, who believed the Chinese were the most supremely rational beings, thought they had been perverted by that "accursed idol."

The classification of idolaters, like other all-purpose pejoratives (lately, terrorists), did not encourage distinctions. In India, this figure was one god in a crowd of monkey gods and elephant-headed gods, blue men and women with four arms. Moreover, he existed only in abandoned temples and neglected statuary. Buddhism had vanished from India centuries before, and the native informants, the brahmans, merely knew the Buddha, if at all, from his later absorption into Hinduism as an avatar of Vishnu. Elsewhere in Asia, the religion was thriving, but the Westerners did not realize it was the same religion. They misheard the regional languages and invented names for the different gods—Baouth or Budu, Xaca or Sciacca-Thubba (for Sakyamuni), Sommona-Codom (from the Thai), Fo (from the Chinese), Sagamoni Borcan (from the Mongolian), among hundreds of others—before they slowly discovered that these were not many, but one, and not a god, but an actual, historical man. It was a long path to enlightenment, through many incarnations of bizarre speculations, falsehoods, and half-truths. Although he was first mentioned in the West by St. Clement of Alexandria in the 3rd century, it was not until 1801, according to the *OED*, that the word "Buddha" entered the English language, and some decades after that until the portrait we now consider standard emerged.

Encountering the strange, the Christians naturally fixed on the traces of things that were familiar, inevitably concluding that they were distortions of immutable truth. According to Guy Tachard, a 17th-century French Jesuit, Buddhism was a "monstrous mixture of Christianity and the most ridiculous fables." Both religions had heavens and hells (though the Buddhist ones were multiple and not eternal—merely way-stations on the path to the next incarnation). Both had monks who were celibate, dressed in robes, and collected alms. Both the Buddha (in some versions of the story) and Jesus were born from a virgin birth. The Japanese names for the Buddha's parents, Jōbon Dai Ō and Magabonin were apparent corruptions of Joseph and Mary. Buddhist prayer chants, said Matteo Ricci, sound like Gregorian, and they chant the name Tolome, not knowing that it clearly means that "they wish to honor their cult with the authority of the Apostle Bartholomew." Others thought the Buddha a decayed memory of Thomas the Apostle, who was said to have gone to India after the Resurrection. Some assumed the Buddhists were a branch of the Nestorian Christians who, exiled from Constantinople in the 5th century, had fled to Persia and later flourished in Tang Dynasty China and among the Mongols. Protestants like Samuel Purchas found the Buddhist monasteries in Ceylon "Popish, being also gilded with gold," with "saints" in their "chapels," "set on the Altars" "clothed with garments of gold and silver." "Any man that should see it," he wrote, "would think our Western Monks had hence borrowed their Ceremonies."

Francis Xavier—whose source was an accommodating, illiterate, renegade Japanese wanted for murder, whom he met in Malacca in 1547—initially believed that the Buddha was not an idol but, like Moses, had ordered the smashing of idols in the name of the One God. Two years later, when he arrived in Japan, Xavier changed his mind, calling the Buddha "the pure invention of demons." Trying to teach the Japanese the truth, he transformed the Latin *deus* into the Japanese *daiusu*, which unfortunately sounded like *dai usō*, a big lie.

For their part, the Asians also looked for the familiar in these mysterious visitors. Some thought the Jesuits were Buddhist monks from India, but they couldn't understand why these men would wear an image of Devadatta around their necks. (Devadatta was the Buddha's evil nemesis, who tried to assassinate him on various occasions, and ended up in the worst of the sixteen hells, impaled on stakes.) It must mean that these men in robes were some sort of anti-Buddhist cult—in Western terms, Satanists.

In the 17th century, with the opening of trade routes and the presence of Westerners living in Asia and learning the languages, it was finally understood that this idol was the same person in all the countries. But, in the perennial belief that ancient people in barbaric lands could never have created anything without guidance from the more advanced—in modern times this is usually attributed to Atlanteans or extraterrestrials—it could not be imagined that the Asians had elaborated this complex religion on their own. Buddhism had to have come from one of the civilized, however idolatrous, countries—namely, Egypt. Engelbert Kaempfer, who spent years in Asia with the Dutch East India Company, and whose accounts were influential into the 18th century, declared that the Buddha was a priest from Memphis, expelled by the Persian conquest of Egypt in the mid-6th century BCE, who had fled to India taking with him not only the doctrine of the transmigration of souls, but the worship of cows (like the Egyptian god Apis) and animal-headed gods. Moreover, because of the "wooly curls" on his head, it was obvious that the Buddha was a Negro. Various British residents in India, including the great Sir William Jones, discoverer of the Indo-European language roots, echoed this: The Buddha had the nose and lips and the "crisp and wooly" hair of Ethiopians. (Others, however, thought that the curls on the Buddha's head were snails.)

Athanasius Kircher, whose name is always followed with the epithet The Last Man Who Knew Everything—including the knowledge that the entirety of Chinese civilization came from Egypt, proven by their "hieroglyphic" writing—also believed that the Buddha was originally a priest of Osiris. "He was a very sinful brahman imbued with Pythagoreanism," (that is, a belief in reincarnation, not otherwise shared by the priests of Osiris), "an "impostor known all over the East," who "infected the whole Orient with his pestilent dogmas."

Kaempfer, in what became a popular theory, thought there were two Buddhas: the real one who had lived many thousands of years ago, and the Egyptian priest, who was an impostor claiming to be him. Kircher and Kaempfer were modified by the Augustinian friar Antonio Agostino Giorgi, who moved the chronology one step forward: The first Buddha was the priest of Osiris, but the second was a Gnostic or Manichean who came to India after the resurrection of Christ, pretending to be Jesus.

Sir William Jones's discovery of the Indo-European family of languages led to speculations on the mythological connections, and it soon became difficult to sort out which deity was actually, or pretending to be, whom. Louis-Mathieu Langlès, curator of Oriental manuscripts at the Bibliothèque Nationale under Napoleon, declared that the Buddha was also the Egyptian Thoth, the Scandinavian Woden, the Roman Mercury, the Greek Hermes, as well as some gods from Lapland and the Tungus. The Rev. George Stanley Faber, a preacher at Oxford in the early 19th century, added to the list Adam, Noah, the patriarch Enoch, Janus, Hercules, and the Cyclops. Moreover, he argued, since "Buddha and Woden are the same deity . . . the theology of the Gothic and Saxon tribes was a modification of Buddhism." Mindfulness, no doubt, spurred on by horns of mead.

The absence of Buddhists in India, and the (historically false) presumption that they were driven out by the brahmans led to a kinder view of the Buddha among some of the legions of amateur scholars in the East India Company and later the colonial government. Most of them were Protestants, and the austerity of the Buddha made him a kind of Calvin to the Papist excess of Hinduism they saw around them. Buddhism, after all, had eliminated all those strange gods and venerated humans who had achieved enlightenment. And it was known that the Buddha had opposed two practices which repelled the British: animal sacrifices and the caste system. A few of the colonialists speculated on what a different place India would be if it were still Buddhist. This Buddhism would, of course, be a pure form, unlike that which was practiced in the neighboring countries where, they assumed, it had become corrupted by mixing with native beliefs and rituals.

This emergence of a sympathetic Buddha—or what might be called Buddhist compassion toward Buddhists—was finally brought about in the West by the reading and translation of actual Buddhist texts, a contrast to the bits of contradictory information gathered from native informants. Among the scholars was Julius Heinrich Klaproth, son of the discoverer of uranium, whose 1824 life of the Buddha, based on Mongolian texts, stated that "No other religion, other than that of Jesus Christ, has contributed as much to the betterment of men than that of *Bouddha*. . . . The fierce nomads of Central Asia were changed by it into soft and virtuous men. . . ." Alexander Csoma de Kőrös, searching for the origins of his Hungarian language, ended up spending many years in a tiny, unheated room in Ladakh, wrapped in sheepskins and translating Tibetan works. (In the 1930s, the Japanese officially recognized him as a boddhisattva.) George Turnour in Ceylon was translating Pāli texts in order to write, in 1837, the most detailed biography of "Gotamó Buddho" to date. Turnour's aim was to prove the historical verity of the Buddha, whom he nonetheless considered a "wonderful impostor" who had promulgated "intentional perversion and mystification."

In Kathmandu, Brian Houghton Hodgson was stranded for years with little to do for his employer, the East India Company, and passed the time collecting ornithological specimens for the British Museum and Buddhist scriptures. The original, Sanskrit versions of Buddhist texts had been lost in India, and were only known to exist in translations into Chinese, Tibetan, Pāli, Mongolian, and other languages. Hodgson had found them among the Newars, a Buddhist community in otherwise Hindu Nepal. Many of the books he sent to Eugène Burnouf in Paris. Burnouf, a professor who never visited Asia and never met a Buddhist, had moved from his studies of Avestan, the sacred language of the Zoroastrians, to Sanskrit, having caught from German Romanticism the fever of the time: a passionate belief that, as the study of Greek and Roman antiquity had brought on the Renaissance, so the knowledge of India would transform modern times.

Burnouf was the greatest Sanskrit scholar of the period, and his translations of the texts Hodgson sent—including the most influential of Buddhist texts, the *Lotus Sutra*—and his vast *Introduction to the History of Indian Buddhism* was a book read by Thoreau, Emerson, Schelling, Schopenhauer, Nietzsche, and Wagner (who left notes for an unwritten "Buddhist" opera at his death), among many others. Bernouf's Buddha was neither idol nor god, but the teacher of a humanist philosophy that, unlike the Hindu caste system, offered a liberation that was available to all. The original Sanskrit texts offered the clearest views of the Buddha's own philosophy—in Bernouf's words, the "most ancient, the human Buddhism." They were, he wrote, "of incontestable value for the history of the human spirit."

It was remarkable how quickly the image of the Buddha had changed. In 1790, Father Paulinus, a Carmelite missionary on the Malabar coast and author of the first European grammar of Sanskrit, had proven that the Buddha was not a man, but the planet Mercury. By the 1840s, the West had more or less the image of the Buddha that we still have today. It was not, however, a complete triumph. Two years after Burnouf's early death in 1852, H. H. Wilson, the leading scholar of Sanskrit in Britain—director of the Royal Asiatic Society, appointed at Oxford to the country's first chair of Sanskrit—lectured that the Buddha was a fraud who had never existed, that "ignorance and superstition" are the "main props of Buddhism," but that fortunately it will be "overturned" by the Christian missionaries, "whose salutary influence civilization is extending." Wilson, almost needless to say, found the admiration of the Buddha typically French.

All of these stories, and many more, are told in Donald S. Lopez's *From Stone to Flesh: A Short History of the Buddha*, which ends with the birth of the "modern" Buddha. Lopez is a lively scholar, always worth reading, but it's hard to keep up with him. He's a translator of Tibetan texts; the general editor of the wonderful Princeton "Religions in Practice" series and the editor of its volumes on China, India, Buddhism, and

Tibet; the general editor of the Chicago "Buddhism and Modernity" series; the editor of books by the Dalai Lama, collections of Buddhist scriptures, and of the book *Curators of the Buddha*, which brought astonishing news about some of the best-known scholars: among them, the great Tibetologist Giuseppe Tucci, dressing up in Fascist uniforms and editing a Buddhist-Fascist magazine during the war, or D. T. Suzuki's Japanese nationalist agenda in promoting Zen to the barbaric West.

Lopez's primary theme, in many of his own writings, is the transmission of Buddhism in the West. His books tend to be an expansion of a chapter or a few pages in a previous book—a lotus within a lotus, to use a traditional image. Thus *Buddhism and Science* (2008), on the applications that have been given of Buddhism to everything from 19th-century racial theories to contemporary neuroscience, leads to *The Scientific Buddha* (2012), which attempts to recuperate Buddhism from science. A chapter in *Prisoners in Shangri-La* (1998), on the Western imagining of Tibet, is expanded into *The Tibetan Book of the Dead: A Biography* (2011), the story of a Theosophist from Trenton, New Jersey, Walt Wentz, who reinvented himself as W. Y. Evans-Wentz. Given some random pages from a Tibetan text by a British officer in Darjeeling, he had them translated by an eccentric local schoolteacher, erected an edifice around it of explication largely derived from Madame Blavatsky, and named the whole shebang after E. Wallis Budge's popular *The Egyptian Book of the Dead*. (In brief, no Tibetan sage ever advised us to turn off our minds, relax, and float downstream.)

A short section in *From Stone to Flesh* has now turned into a book-length study, *In Search of the Christian Buddha*, written with the medievalist Peggy McCracken. It's one of the odder stories in literary and religious history; as the book's subtitle puts it: *How an Asian Sage Became a Medieval Saint.*

The biography of the Buddha, formalized centuries after his death, is well known. At the birth of Prince Siddhartha, the astrologers declare that he will either become a great ruler or renounce the world and become a Buddha. His father, afraid that Siddhartha will discover the sorrows of the world and abandon it, raises the child in a sealed-off pleasure palace where everyone is young and beautiful. At twenty-nine, curious about life, Siddhartha sneaks out of the palace and makes four trips on his chariot, one in each direction. He sees things he never knew existed: an old man, a sick man, a corpse. On the fourth trip he meets a mendicant and resolves to join him. Siddhartha's father, the king, tries to keep the prince in the palace by sending him beautiful women to play and dance for him. He is not tempted, escapes, and spends the next six years wandering and practicing terrible austerities. He finally renounces those austerities, and sits under the bodhi tree where, resisting final temptations from Mara, the god of death and desire, he achieves enlightenment. He then goes out in the world to teach the Four Noble Truths: the existence and cause of suffering and the path to the end of suffering. Siddhartha and his father are reconciled; the king accepts the Buddha.

Probably in the 8th century in Baghdad, an Arabic version of the story, *The Book of Bilawar and Budhasaf*, appeared, probably translated from a lost Persian text. Set in India, the prince Budhasaf (Arabic for "bodhisattva"), on leaving the palace, acquires a teacher, Bilawar, who has come from Sarandib (Ceylon) to instruct him with maxims and parables, many drawn from Buddhism, including the famous one of the caskets (covered in gold but containing trash inside or covered in pitch but containing gold) that would later turn up in *The Merchant of Venice*. Budhasaf's father is a persecutor of the "religion," which has no resemblance to Buddhism, and the father-son relation is contentious. In the end, after many twists and palace debates, the father renounces his idols to follow the son's ascetic religion. There is no bodhi tree and no Noble Truths, but the rest of the story is generally the same. The mendicant, however, whom Siddhartha in the end did not follow—having chosen to wander alone—has now become a major character as the prince's teacher.

The Arabic version was then Christianized and translated into Georgian as the *Balavariani* by monks in the Monastery of St. Sabas in Palestine in the 9th or 10th century. Budhasaf is named Iodasaph, his teacher Bilawar is now Balahvar; the "religion" is the monks' own Christian asceticism. The king is a ruthless suppressor of Christians, but finally converts. Iodasaph has "released the race of Indians by God's power from their benighted devil-worship."

The Georgian was translated into Greek in the 11th century, possibly by Euthymius the Iberian on Mount Athos, as *Barlaam and Iosaph*, with a great deal of theological exegesis and scriptural citations added. Quite soon after, the Greek was translated into Latin by monks in Amalfi. Their version, *Barlaam and Josaphat*, spread throughout Christendom and was adapted, in one form or another, into Spanish, Catalan, Occitan, Italian, English, High and Low German, Dutch, and Bohemian. There were ten versions in French alone, and one of them, a heavily didactic 13th-century rendition in verse by Gui de Cambrai has recently been translated for Penguin Classics by McCracken, Lopez's co-author. The setting is still India, but the king is a "Saracen," despite being in India, and father and son must go to holy war before the father relents. The Buddha had become a Crusader.

Barlaam and Josaphat finally achieved absolute stardom when their tale was retold in Jacobus de Voragine's collection of saints, *The Golden Legend*—for centuries the most popular book in the West, outselling the Bible after the invention of printed books. And there was even a Jewish version, translated into Hebrew directly from the Arabic in al-Andalus by Abraham ibn Hasday in 1240, complete with Talmudic emendations. Called *The Book of the Prince and the Hermit*, it would be translated into German and Yiddish in the 18th and 19th centuries.

The two saints were included in Pope Gregory XIII's *Roman Martyrology* in 1583 for their "wondrous deeds" "among the Indians, near the Persian boundary." A few years later, the Jesuits brought a printing press to Japan, and among their first books was a *Compendium of the Acts of the Saints*, which included a Japanese translation of the complete *Barlaam and Josaphat*. There are no surviving records of how the Japanese felt about having familiar stories of the Buddha employed to convert them away from Buddhism.

It's a modernist tale: A true (or presumably true) story turns into fiction, travels through many centuries and many languages and ends up almost where it began, still more or less the same while simultaneously having turned into its opposite. And even stranger, the fiction had become real. In 1571, the doge of Venice presented a sacred relic to King Sebastian of Portugal: a bone from Josaphat's spine. It is still in a silver reliquary in the St. Andrieskerk in Antwerp.

The "I Ching"

The *I Ching* has served for thousands of years as a philosophical taxonomy of the universe, a guide to an ethical life, a manual for rulers, and an oracle of one's personal future and the future of the state. It was an organizing principle or authoritative proof for literary and arts criticism, cartography, medicine, and many of the sciences, and it generated endless Confucian, Taoist, Buddhist, and, later, even Christian commentaries, and competing schools of thought within those traditions. In China and in East Asia, it has been by far the most consulted of all books, in the belief that it can explain everything. In the West, it has been known for over three hundred years and, since the 1950s, is surely the most popularly recognized Chinese book. With its seeming infinitude of applications and interpretations, there has never been a book quite like it anywhere. It is the center of a vast whirlwind of writings and practices, but is itself a void, or perhaps a continually shifting cloud, for most of the key words of the *I Ching* have no fixed meaning.

The origin of the text is, as might be expected, obscure. In the mythological version, the culture hero Fu Hsi, a dragon or a snake with a human face, studied the patterns of nature in the sky and on the earth: the markings on birds, rocks, and animals, the movement of clouds, the arrangement of the stars. He discovered that everything could be reduced to eight trigrams, each composed of three stacked solid or broken lines. The lines reflected the *yin* and *yang*, the duality that drives the universe, and the trigrams themselves represented, respectively, heaven, a lake, fire, thunder, wind, water, a mountain, and earth. From these building blocks of the cosmos, Fu Hsi devolved all aspects of civilization—kingship, marriage, writing, navigation, agriculture—all of which he taught to his human descendants.

Here mythology turns into legend: Around the year 1050 BCE, according to the tradition, the Emperor Wen, founder of the Chou dynasty, doubled the trigrams to hexagrams (six-lined figures), numbered and arranged all of the possible combinations—there are sixty-four—and gave them names. He wrote brief oracles for each that have since been known as the "Judgments." His son, the Duke of Chou, a poet, added gnomic interpretations for the individual lines of each hexagram, known simply as the "Lines." It was said that, five hundred years later, Confucius himself wrote ethical commentaries explicating each hexagram, which are called the "Ten Wings" ("wing," that is, in the architectural sense).

The archeological and historical version of this narrative is far murkier. In the Shang dynasty (which began circa 1600 BCE) or possibly even earlier, fortune-telling diviners would apply heat to tortoise shells or the scapulae of oxen and interpret the cracks that were produced. Many of these "oracle bones"—hundreds of thousands of them have been unearthed—have complete hexagrams or the numbers assigned to hexagrams incised on them. Where the hexagrams came from, or how they were interpreted, is completely unknown.

Sometime in the Chou dynasty—the current guess is around 800 BCE—the sixty-four hexagrams were named, and a written text was established, based on the oral traditions. The book became known as the *Chou I*, the *Chou Changes*. The process of consultation also evolved from the tortoise shells, which required an expert to perform and interpret, to the system of coins or yarrow stalks that anyone could do and which has been in use ever since. Three coins, with numbers assigned to heads or tails, were simultaneously tossed; the resulting sum indicated a solid or broken line; six coin tosses thus produced a hexagram. In the case of the yarrow stalks, fifty were counted out in a more laborious procedure to produce the number for each line.

By the 3rd century BCE, with the rise of Confucianism, the "Ten Wings" commentaries had been added, transforming the *Chou I* from a strictly divinatory manual to a philosophical and ethical text. In 136

BCE, Emperor Wu of the Han dynasty declared it the most important of the five canonical Confucian books and standardized the text
from among various competing versions (some with the hexagrams
in a different order). It became the *I Ching*, the *Book* (or *Classic*) *of
Change*, and its format has remained the same since: a named and
numbered hexagram, an arcane "Judgment" for that hexagram, an
often poetic interpretation of the image obtained by the combination
of the two trigrams, and enigmatic statements on the meaning of
each line of the hexagram. Confucius almost certainly had nothing
to do with the making of the *I Ching*, but he did supposedly say that if
he had another hundred years to live, fifty of them would be devoted
to studying it.

For two millennia, the *I Ching* was the essential guide to the universe. In a philosophical cosmos where everything is connected
and everything is in a state of restless change, the book was not a
description of the universe but rather its most perfect microcosm.
It represented, as one Sinologist has put it, the "underpinnings of
reality." Its sixty-four hexagrams became the irrevocable categories
for countless disciplines. Its mysterious "Judgments" were taken as
kernels of thought to be elaborated, in the "Ten Wings" and libraries
of commentaries, into advice to rulers on how to run an orderly state
and to ordinary people on how to live a proper life. It was a tool for
meditation on the cosmos and, as a seamless piece of the way of the
world, it also knew what would be auspicious or inauspicious for the
future.

In the West, the *I Ching* was discovered in the late 17th century by
Jesuit missionaries in China, who decoded the text to reveal its Christian universal truth: hexagram number one was God; two was the
second Adam, Jesus; three was the Trinity; eight was the members of
Noah's family; and so on. Leibniz enthusiastically found the universality of his binary system in the solid and broken lines. Hegel—who
thought Confucius was not worth translating—considered the book

"superficial": "There is not to be found in one single instance a sensuous conception of universal natural or spiritual powers."

The first English translation was done by Canon Thomas McClatchie, an Anglican cleric in Hong Kong. McClatchie was a Reverend Casaubon figure who, in 1876, four years after the publication of *Middlemarch*, found the key to all mythologies and asserted that the *I Ching* had been brought to China by one of Noah's sons and was a pornographic celebration of a "hermaphroditic monad," elsewhere worshiped among the Chaldeans as Baal and among Hindus as Shiva. James Legge, also a missionary in Hong Kong and, despite a general loathing of China, the first important English-language translator of the Chinese classics, considered McClatchie "delirious." After twenty interrupted years of work—the manuscript was lost in a shipwreck in the Red Sea—Legge produced the first somewhat reliable English translation of the *I Ching* in 1882, and the one that first applied the English word for a six-pointed star, "hexagram," to the Chinese block of lines.

Professionally appalled by its "idolatry" and "superstition," Legge nevertheless found himself "gradually brought under a powerful fascination," and it led him to devise a novel theory of translation. Since Chinese characters were not, he claimed, "representations of words, but symbols of ideas," therefore the "combination of them in composition is not a representation of what the writer would say, but of what he thinks." The translator, then, must become *"en rapport"* with the author, a "seeing of mind to mind," a "participation" in the thoughts of the author that goes beyond what the author merely said. Although the *I Ching* has no author, Legge's version is flooded with explanations and clarifications parenthetically inserted into an otherwise literal translation of the text.

Herbert Giles, the next important English-language translator after Legge, thought the *I Ching* was "apparent gibberish": "This is freely admitted by all learned Chinese, who nevertheless hold tenaciously to the belief that important lessons could be derived from its pages if only we had the wit to understand them." Arthur Waley, in a 1933 study—he never translated the entire book—described it as a collection of "peasant interpretation" omens to which specific divinations had been added at a later date. Thus, taking a familiar Western example, he wrote that the omen "red sky in the morning, shepherds take warning" would become the divination "red sky in the morning: inauspicious; do not cross the river." Waley proposed three categories of omens—"inexplicable sensations and involuntary movements ('feelings,' twitchings, stumbling, belching, and the like); those concerning plants, animals, and birds; [and] those concerning natural phenomena (thunder, stars, rain, etc.)"—and found examples of all of them in his decidedly unmetaphysical reading of the book. Joseph Needham devoted many exasperated pages to the *I Ching* in *Science and Civilization in China* as a "pseudo-science" that had, for centuries, a deleterious effect on actual Chinese science, which attempted to fit exact observations of the natural and physical worlds into the "cosmic filing-system" of the vague categories of the hexagrams.

It was Richard Wilhelm's 1924 German translation of the *I Ching* and especially the English translation of the German by the Jungian Cary F. Baynes in 1950 that transformed the text from Sinological arcana to international celebrity. Wilhelm, like Legge, was a missionary in China, but unlike Legge was an ardent believer in the Wisdom of the East, with China the wisest of all. The "relentless mechanization and rationalization of life in the West" needed the "Eastern adhesion to a natural profundity of soul." His mission was to "join hands in mutual completion," to uncover the "common foundations of humankind" in order to "find a core in the innermost depth of the humane, from where we can tackle the shaping of life."

Wilhelm's translation relied heavily on late, Sung Dynasty Neo-Confucian interpretations of the text. In the name of universality, specifically Chinese referents were given general terms, and the German edition had scores of footnotes noting "parallels" to

Goethe, Kant, the German Romantics, and the Bible. (These were dropped for the English-language edition.) The text was oddly presented twice: the first time with short commentaries, the second time with more extended ones. The commentaries were undifferentiated amalgams of various Chinese works and Wilhelm's own meditations. (Needham thought that the edition belonged to the "Department of Utter Confusion": "Wilhelm seems to be the only person . . . who knew what this was all about.") The book carried an introduction by Carl Jung, whom Wilhelm considered "in touch with the findings of the East [and] in accordance with the views of the oldest Chinese wisdom." (One proof was Jung's male and female principles, the *anima* and the *animus*, which Wilhelm connected to *yin* and *yang*.) Some of Jung's assertions are now embarrassing ("It is a curious fact that such a gifted and intelligent people as the Chinese have never developed what we call science"), but his emphasis on chance—or synchronicity, the Jungian, metaphysical version of chance—as the guiding principle for a sacred book was, at the time, something unexpected, even if, for true believers, the *I Ching* does not operate on chance at all.

The Wilhelm/Baynes Bollingen edition was a sensation in the 1950s and 1960s. Octavio Paz, Allen Ginsberg, Jorge Luis Borges, and Charles Olson, among many others, wrote poems inspired by its poetic language. Fritjof Capra in *The Tao of Physics* used it to explain quantum mechanics and Terence McKenna found that its geometrical patterns mirrored the "chemical waves" produced by hallucinogens. Others considered its binary system of lines a prototype for the computer. Philip K. Dick and Raymond Queneau based novels on it; Jackson Mac Low and John Cage invented elaborate procedures using it to generate poems and musical compositions. It is not difficult to recuperate how thrilling the arrival of the *I Ching* was to the avant-gardists, who were emphasizing process over product in art, and to the anti-authoritarian counterculturalists. It brought, not from the soulless West, but from the Mysterious East, what Wilhelm

145

called "the seasoned wisdom of thousands of years." It was an ancient book without an author, a cyclical configuration with no beginning or end, a religious text with neither exotic gods nor priests to whom one must submit, a do-it-yourself divination that required no professional diviner. It was a self-help book for those who wouldn't be caught reading self-help books, and moreover one that provided an alluring glimpse of one's personal future. It was, said Bob Dylan, "the only thing that is amazingly true."

The two latest translations of the *I Ching* couldn't be more unalike; they are a complementary *yin* and *yang* of approaches. John Minford is a scholar best known for his work on the magnificent five-volume translation of *The Story of the Stone (The Dream of the Red Chamber)*, universally considered the greatest Chinese novel, in a project begun by the late David Hawkes. His *I Ching*, obviously the result of many years of study, is nine hundred pages long, much of it in small type, and encyclopedic. Minford presents two complete translations: the "Bronze Age Oracle," a recreation of the Chou dynasty text before any of the later Confucian commentaries were added to it, and the "Book of Wisdom," the text as it was elucidated in the subsequent centuries. Each portion of the entries for each hexagram is accompanied by an exegesis that is a digest of the historical commentaries and the interpretations by previous translators, as well as reflections by Minford himself that link the hexagram to Chinese poetry, art, ritual, history, philosophy, and mythology. It is a tour-de-force of erudition, almost a microcosm of Chinese civilization, much as the way the *I Ching* itself was traditionally seen.

David Hinton is, with Arthur Waley and Burton Watson, the rare example of a literary Sinologist—that is, a classical scholar thoroughly conversant with, and connected to, contemporary literature in English. A generation younger than Watson, he and Watson are surely the most important American translators of Chinese classical poetry and philosophy in the last fifty years. Both are immensely prolific, both have introduced entirely new ways of translating Chinese poetry. Hinton's *I Ching* is equally inventive. It is quite short, with only two pages allotted to each hexagram, and presents a few excerpts from the original "Ten Wings" commentaries, but has nothing further from Hinton himself, other than a short introduction. Rather than consulted, it is meant to be read cover to cover, like a book of modern poetry—though it should be quickly said that this is very much a translation, and not an "imitation" or a postmodern elaboration. Or perhaps its fragments and aphorisms are meant to be dipped into at random, the way one reads E. M. Cioran or Elias Canetti.

Hinton adheres to a Taoist or Ch'an (Zen) Buddhist reading of the book, unconcerned with the Confucian ethical and political interpretations. His *I Ching* puts the reader into the Tao of nature: that is, the way of the world as it is exemplified by nature and embodied by the book. He takes the mysterious lines of the judgments as precursors to the later Taoist and Ch'an writings: "strategies to tease the mind outside workaday assumptions and linguistic structures, outside the limitations of identity." The opposite of Wilhelm's Jungian self-realization, it is intended as a realization of selflessness. Moreover, it is based on the belief that archaic Chinese culture, living closer to the land—and a land that still had a great deal of wilderness—was less estranged from nature's Tao. To that end, Hinton occasionally translates according to a pictographic reading of the oldest characters, a technique first used by Ezra Pound in his idiosyncratic and wonderful version of the earliest poetry anthology, the *Book of Songs*, which he titled *The Confucian Odes*. For example, Hinton calls Hexagram 32—usually translated as "Endurance" or "Duration" or "Perseverance"—"Moondrift Constancy," because the character portrays a half-moon fixed in place with a line above and below it. The character for "observation" becomes "heron's-eye gaze," for indeed it has a heron and an eye in it, and nothing watches more closely than a waterbird. Hinton doesn't do this kind of pictographic reading often, but no doubt Sinologists will be scandalized.

The difference between the two translations—the differences among all translations—is apparent if we look at a single hexagram: number 52, called *Ken*. Minford translates the name as "Mountain," for the hexagram is composed of the two Mountain trigrams, one on top of the other. His translation of the text throughout the book is minimalist, almost telegraphese, with each line centered, rather than flush left. He has also made the exceedingly strange decision to incorporate tags in Latin, taken from the early Jesuit translations, which he claims "can help us relate to this deeply ancient and foreign text, can help create a timeless mood of contemplation, and at the same time can evoke indirect connections between the Chinese traditions of Self-Knowledge and Self-Cultivation . . . and the long European tradition of Gnosis and spiritual discipline." In the "Book of Wisdom" section, he translates the "Judgment" for hexagram 52 as:

> The back
> Is still
> As a mountain;
> There is no body.
> He walks
> In the courtyard,
> Unseen.
> No Harm,
> *Nullum malum.*

This is followed by a long and interesting exegesis on the spiritual role and poetic image of mountains in the Chinese tradition.

Hinton calls the hexagram "Stillness" and translates into prose: "Stillness in your back. Expect nothing from your life. Wander the courtyard where you see no one. How could you ever go astray?"

Wilhelm has "Keeping Still, Mountain" as the name of the hexagram. His "Judgment" reads:

KEEPING STILL. Keeping his back still
So that he no longer feels his body.
He goes into the courtyard
And does not see his people.
No blame.

He explains:

> True quiet means keeping still when the time has come to keep
> still, and going forward when the time has come to go forward.
> In this way rest and movement are in agreement with the de-
> mands of the time, and thus there is light in life. The hexagram
> signifies the end and beginning of all movement. The back is
> named because in the back are located all the nerve fibers that
> mediate movement. If the movement of these spinal nerves is
> brought to a standstill, the ego, with its restlessness, disappears
> as it were. When a man has thus become calm, he may turn to
> the outside world. He no longer sees in it the struggle and tu-
> mult of individual beings, and therefore he has that true peace
> of mind which is needed for understanding the great laws of the
> universe and for acting in harmony with them. Whoever acts
> from these deep levels makes no mistakes.

The Columbia University Press *I Ching*, translated by Richard
John Lynn and billed as the "definitive version" "after decades of inaccurate translations," has "Restraint" for *Ken*: "Restraint takes place
with the back, so does not obtain [*sic*] the other person. He goes into
that one's courtyard but does not see him there. There is no blame."
Lynn's odd explanation, based on the Han Dynasty commentator
Wang Bi, is that if two people have their backs turned, "even if they
are close, they do not see each other." Therefore neither restrains the
other and each exercises self-restraint.

The six judgments for the six individual lines of Hexagram 52
travel through the body, including the feet, calves, waist, trunk, and
jaws. (Wilhelm, weirdly and ahistorically speculates that "possibly

the words of the text embody directions for the practice of yoga.") Thus, for line 2, Hinton has: "Stillness fills your calves. Raise up succession, all that will follow you, or you'll never know contentment."

Minford translates it as: "The calves are / Still as a Mountain. / Others / Are not harnessed. / The heart is heavy." He explains: "There is a potential healing, a Stillness. But the Energy of Others ... cannot be mastered and harnessed. No Retreat is possible, only a reluctant acceptance. One lacks the foresight for Retreat. Beware."

Wilhelm's version is: "Keeping his calves still. / He cannot rescue him whom he follows. / His heart is not glad." This is glossed as:

> The leg cannot move independently; it depends on the movement of the body. If a leg is suddenly stopped while the whole body is in vigorous motion, the continuing body movement will make one fall. The same is true of a man who serves a master stronger than himself. He is swept along, and even though he himself may halt on the path of wrongdoing, he can no longer check the other in his powerful movement. When the master presses forward, the servant, no matter how good his intentions, cannot save him.

In the "Bronze Age Oracle" section—the original Chou book without the later interpretations—Minford translates *Ken* as "Tending," believing that it refers to traditional medicine and the need to tend the body. The "Judgment" for the entire hexagram reads: "The back / Is tended. / The body / Unprotected. / He walks / In an empty courtyard. / No harm." He suggests that the "empty courtyard" is a metaphor for the whole body, left untended. His judgement for the second line is: "The calves / Are tended. / There is / No strength / In the flesh. / The heart / Is sad," which he glosses as "There is not enough flesh on the calves. Loss of weight is a concern, and it directly affects the emotions."

Both Richard J. Smith, in a monograph on the *I Ching* for the Princeton "Lives of Great Religious Books" series, and Arthur Waley take the hexagram back to the prevalent practice in the Shang Dynasty of human and animal sacrifice. Smith translates *Ken* as "cleave" (but, in an entirely different reading, says that the word might also mean "to glare at"). His "Judgment" is puzzling: "If one cleaves the back he will not get hold of the body; if one goes into the courtyard he will not see the person. There will be no misfortune." But his reading of line two is graphic: "Cleave the lower legs, but don't remove the bone marrow. His heart is not pleased."

Waley thinks *Ken* means "gnawing," and "evidently deals with omen-taking according to the way in which rats, mice or the like have deals with the body of the sacrificial victim when exposed as 'bait' to the ancestral spirit." His "Judgment" is: "If they have gnawed its back, but not possessed themselves of the body, / It means that you will go to a man's house, but not find him at home." He reads line 2 as: "If they gnaw the calf of the leg, but don't pull out the bone marrow, their (i.e. the ancestors') hearts do not rejoice."

What is certain is that Hexagram 52 is composed of two Mountain trigrams and has something to do with the back and something to do with a courtyard that is either empty or where the people in it are not seen. Otherwise, these few lines may be about stillness, having no expectations, self-restraint, peace of mind, knowing when not to follow a leader, the care of various aches and pains, glaring at things, and the preparations for, and results of, human or animal sacrifices.

None of these are necessarily misinterpretations or mistranslations. One could say that the *I Ching* is a mirror of one's own concerns or expectations. But it's like one of the bronze mirrors from the Shang Dynasty, now covered in a dark blue-green patina so that it doesn't reflect at all. Minford recalls that in his last conversation with David Hawkes, the dying master-scholar told him: "Be sure to let your readers know that every sentence can be read in an almost infinite number of ways! That is the secret of the book. No one will ever know what it *really* means." In the *I Ching*, the same word means both "war prisoner" and "sincerity."

American Indias

Thou hast there in thy wrist a Sanskrit charge
To conjugate infinity's dim marge—
Anew ...!

—Hart Crane, *The Bridge*

We in the US inhabit a misplaced India, the land that Columbus thought he had found. Half a millennium later, the descendants of the original occupants are still bizarrely called Indians, no doubt because it has proven useful for the immigrants to treat the locals as foreigners. But if the story of Indian America is a huge and largely tragic epic, alongside it is a little anthology of lyrics, idiosyncratic moments: the invention of American Indias.

The mega-bestseller in the colonies, first published in 1751 and reprinted fifty-four times, was *The Economy of Human Life: Translated from an Indian Manuscript Written by an Ancient Brahmin*. This "ancient book" had been given by a lama in the Potala in Lhasa to a Chinese official named Caotsou, a man "of grave and noble aspect, of great eloquence," who translated it from the Sanskrit ("though, as he himself confesses, with an utter incapacity for reaching, in the Chinese language, the strength and sublimity of the original"). Translated from Chinese into English by an unknown hand, the book presented the "Oriental System of Morality" in a series of maxims on modesty, prudence, piety, and temperance, that seemed to emanate more from a Calvinist pulpit than the environs of an adorned lingam: "The first step to being wise is to know that thou are ignorant"; "The terrors of death are no terrors to the good'; "Take unto thyself a wife and become a faithful member of society"; "Keep the desires of thy heart within the bounds of moderation"; "Receive not a favor from the hand of the proud."

[The book, now believed to be the work of an English bibliophile named Robert Dodsley, had a curious afterlife. It was reprinted verbatim in 1925 by a group of California Rosicrucians as *Unto Thee I Grant,* the "Secret Wisdom of Tibet," which had been transmitted to the Himalayas by the Pharaoh Amenhotep IV (Akhenaten—perennial occultist source of the world's religions). The text, in turn, became part of the ultra-secret *Circle 7 Koran* of the inner-city Moorish Science Temple, which was founded in Newark in 1913 by the prophet Noble Drew Ali (born Timothy Drew) and relocated to Chicago in the 1920s. Among the initiates of the *Circle 7 Koran* were Wallace Fard and Elijah Muhammad, who eventually adapted the sacred knowledge to create the Nation of Islam. There is a line, then, however jagged, from pseudo-Hinduism to Malcolm X.]

Actual artifacts from India began to arrive in New England with the opening of the India trade in 1784: muslins, Bengal ginghams and paisley shawls, monkeys and parrots, tamarind and ginger, knicknacks and small statues of the uncanny gods. The first real Indian—a Tamil from Madras, with a "soft countenance" but "well-proportioned body"—showed up in 1790; six years later, the first elephant, named Old Bet, was a sensation. The East Marine Society, made up of sailors who had been to Asia, had a spectacular annual parade in Salem, with a "palanquin borne by Negroes dressed in the Indian manner."

Intellectual Indophilia begins with both global trade and Sir William Jones's discovery of the Indo-European roots of many languages, the realization that those strange others were somehow part of "us." Samuel Adams, in his retirement devouring books on the East, wrote to Jefferson that "Indeed Newton himself, appears to have discovered nothing that was not known to the Ancient Indians. He has only furnished more ample demonstrations of the doctrines they taught." Post-Revolutionary America's belief in (if not practice of) universal human rights was leading to a preoccupation with a universal human religion. One of the responses was Unitarianism, which found a bridge between the seemingly dissimilar Hinduism and Christianity in the figure of Rammohun Roy, who translated some of the Vedas and the Upanishads and founded the Brahmo Samaj, devoted to recuperating an imagined monotheistic ur-Hinduism, sweeping away the million gods. When Roy moved to London and converted to Christianity (or more exactly, the universal Hindu-Christianity) he became a Unitarian star.

Roy was read by Emerson, who said that India "makes Europe appear the land of trifles." In the Vedas, the *Bhagavad-Gita*, and the *Vishnu Purana*, he found the "highest expression" of the "conception of the fundamental Unity." His philosophical terms, the Over-Soul and the Higher Self, are plainly derived from the Hindu *Brahman* and *atman*; his versions of "illusion" and "fate" come from *maya* and *karma*. Curiously, though his beloved aunt sent him Sanskrit poems and he himself extensively adapted poems by Hafiz, Saadi, and other Persian and Arabic poets, Indian poetry didn't enter into his Indo-worldview and India only appears twice in his poetry: a lament for dead New England farmers, mysteriously titled "Hamatreya," (a word otherwise unknown, though possibly derived from Maitreya, the future Buddha, which doesn't illuminate the poem) and the often-anthologized "Brahma" ("If the red slayer think he slays, / Or if the slain think he is slain, / They know not well the subtle ways / I keep, and pass, and turn again."), a poem that eerily seems indeed to come from the future: the voice of another Indophile, Yeats.

Thoreau discovered India through Emerson, and surpassed him in unqualified enthusiasm: "I cannot read a sentence in the book of the Hindoos [probably either the *Laws of Manu* or the *Bhagavad-Gita*] without being elevated as upon the table-land of the Ghauts. It has such a rhythm as the winds of the desert, such a tide as the Ganges, and seems as superior to criticism as the Himmaleh Mounts." He took the *Gita* with him to Walden and declared himself a yogi. (Some have seen his retreat to the pond as an act of yogic austerity, though his sisters often brought him cookies.) He was given a large library of

154

Indian books, for which, typically, he built a special bookcase out of driftwood, and translated from the French some Buddhist texts and a story from the *Mahabharata*. But he was apparently untempted by the poetry, though he said that Indian "philosophy and poesy seem to me superior to, if not transcending greatly, all others." His enduring contribution to the Indo-American loop is, of course, his "civil disobedience," which inspired Gandhi's *satyagraha*, which inspired Martin Luther King's non-violent resistance.

Though Emerson called *Leaves of Grass* "a remarkable mixture of the Bhagvat Ghita and the *New York Herald*," though many critics have presented Vedantist readings of Whitman, it is likely that his actual knowledge of India was limited to a few magazine articles. Things Indian are scattered through the work, but merely as items in his human catalog; the "Hindu" aspects probably derive from intuition or experience or Emerson. "Passage to India," beyond its famously recycled title, is a celebration of the simultaneous opening in 1869 of both the Suez canal and the transcontinental railroad as a metaphor for the joining of the Old and New Worlds, East and West, the past and the present, and—"Passage to more than India!"—for the soul's voyage into the ether. Apart from a few lines in the sixth section, India itself barely appears, though the invocation of the "tender and junior Buddha" is irresistible.

In 1893, the World Parliament of Religions in Chicago was dedicated to the dream of a single world religion in the new century and featured the glamorous Swami Vivekananda, the first Indian pop star guru. Vivekananda, like the Brahmo Samaj, preached a Hinduism without gods: the Emersonian uniting of a human soul with the universal consciousness of a universal god. In the wake of his extensive speaking tours and the proliferation of branches of his Vedanta Society, the tabloids were full of stories of respectable Christian housewives suddenly abandoning hearth and home for a life of depravity. The dream of unity, from Vivekananda and the gurus who followed his trail, provoked its nightmare: the Immigration Act of 1917, which prohibited immigration to the US by all Asians except Christian Filipinos, and which remained in place until 1965.

In 1896, Mark Twain was the first American writer of note to actually make the passage to India, spending three months there on his around-the-world tour:

> This is India! The land of dreams and romance, of fabulous wealth and fabulous poverty, of splendor and rags, of palaces and hovels, of famine and pestilence, of genii and giants and Aladdin lamps, of tigers and elephants, the cobra and the jungle, the country of a hundred nations and a hundred tongues, of a thousand religions and two million gods, cradle of the human race, birthplace of human speech, mother of history, grandmother of legend, great-grandmother of tradition, whose yesterdays bear date with the mouldering antiquities of the rest of the nations—the one sole country under the sun that is endowed with an imperishable interest for alien persons, for lettered and ignorant, wise and fool, rich and poor, bond and free, the one land that all men desire to see, and having seen once, by even a glimpse, would not give up that glimpse for all the shows of all the rest of the globe combined.

He wrote that "They are much the most interesting people in the world—and the nearest to being incomprehensible." The Indo-American century ends with his wisecrack: "East is East and West is West, and finally the Twain have met."

Anglo-American modernism exuberantly rummaged through the history of poetry—the Greek anthology, the Tang Dynasty, troubadours and Anglo-Saxon bards, the Metaphysicals, the haiku masters—but oddly never discovered classical Indian lyricism. Eliot's Sanskrit studies at Harvard led only to the famous last line of "The Waste Land." Yeats translated ten of the Upanishads with Shree

Purohit Swami, and dreamed that a modern poet would be inspired to create "some new Upanishad, some new half-Asiatic masterpiece," but apparently was unaware of the non-canonical texts.

Pound was initially wildly enthusiastic about Rabindranath Tagore, whom he met with Yeats in 1912 ("I read these things and wonder why one should go on trying to write") and praised Bengali prosody, though he didn't know the language, as "the most finished and most subtle of any known to us," comparing its "sound unit principle" to that of "the most advanced artists in *vers libre*." He collaborated with a young man named Kali Mohan Ghose—a member of the London branch of the Brahmo Samaj, whom he met through Tagore—and translated a few poems from the Hindi by Kabir, which were published in a Calcutta magazine in 1913. But other than a walk-on in the *Pisan Cantos*, Pound never mentioned Kabir again, nor did he translate or write about other classical Indian poets.

The "invention of China" transformed Anglo-American poetry, but nothing similar happened with India, despite the Indian currents floating around modern poetry. Pound's odd, sophomoric short story in 1916, "Jodindranath Mawhor's Occupation," demonstrated that he'd been reading the *Kama Sutra* and the *Laws of Manu*. He practiced yogic breathing into old age and was a lifelong admirer of the writings of Yogi Ramacharaka (whom he did not know was actually William Walker Atkinson, born in Baltimore), where, among other things, he discovered the vortex that became Vorticism. Madame Blavatsky and Henry Steel Olcott were dead, but the Theosophical Society was not only promoting its quirky mythologies, but also serious scholarship in Hinduism and Buddhism. Theosophy was inescapable, and its ideas were not only known in varying degrees to the poets, they also colored nearly all the writing, scholarly or occult, on Indian religions and philosophies in the first half of the century. (Its creative masterpiece was the invention of the *Tibetan Book of the Dead*.) The great art historian and aesthetician Ananda Coomaraswamy had spurred interest in classical Indian art, and Tagore—whom Pound quickly abandoned—was an international phenomenon, easily the most famous poet in the world.

Yet taste and happenstance worked against Indian poetry. The texts that were widely known—mainly the canonical religious works and Tagore—had no place in the prevailing Imagist aesthetic against rhetoric and abstraction. (In Spanish, however, the young Neruda could plagiarize Tagore with no apparent stylistic rupture.) Nor was there in Sanskrit a figure who could occupy a place similar to that of Arthur Waley in classical Chinese and Japanese: that is, a reputable scholar who was connected to the contemporary literary life and capable of writing translations of interest to non-specialists. (Neither did India have a popular, literary, all-purpose, Western "explainer," as Japan did with Lafcadio Hearn.) And, if the religious-erotic *bhakti* poems were known at all to the poets, it is doubtful they would have done much with them, for the Anglo-American poets, at least on the page, were a prudish bunch, compared to the novelists. Their poetry had no Lady Chatterleys or Molly Blooms; their earth rarely moved. It would be hilarious to imagine Krishna and the *gopis* disporting in Eliot's East Coker or H.D.'s Delphi or Stevens's ordinary evening in New Haven or especially in Robert Frost's snowy woods.

Probably the first significant American poem located in India is Muriel Rukeyser's five-part "Ajanta," included in her 1944 *Beast in View*. Though presented as a "journey" from the first line ("Came in my full youth to the midnight cave"), Rukeyser had never been to India at that time. Five years later, in the prose meditation *The Life of Poetry*, she has a few pages on Ajanta as a metaphor for poetry: "The sensation of space within ourselves is the analogy by which the world is known."

James Laughlin spent two years in India in the early 1950s with the Ford Foundation, advising the new, postcolonial publishers. His verse-memoir *Byways* has an entertaining chapter set in Trivandrum, and his time there led to the publication of many classical and contemporary Indian and India-related books by New Directions, but none of them were lyric poetry.

The one major Indo-American poetry "event" or nexus in the second half of the 20th century was the fourteen months Allen Ginsberg and Peter Orlovsky spent traveling in India in 1962 and 1963, joined for part of the time by Gary Snyder and Joanne Kyger, and the mysterious Hope Savage, all in flight from Cold War USA. This "first encounter" (in the anthropological sense) of American poets and actual India is documented in Ginsberg's journals—one of the masterpieces of Beat prose—Snyder's quite beautiful journal, Kyger's more straightforward journal, and in a brilliant retelling by Deborah Baker, *The Blue Hand*. Ginsberg's involvement with the religious street singers, the Bauls, led to a few translations, and to recordings and tours in the US. Above all, passages in Ginsberg's journals and the uncharacteristically few poems he wrote in India come close to an American *bhakti*: the infinite sights, smells, sounds of India pour through in Whitmanian catalogs, all of them ultimately hallucinatory—sometimes literally drug-induced—and illusory. Snyder, in the "Kali" section of *The Back Country*, written in India, and in many short erotic poems written in the decades since, seems more directly influenced by the actual *bhakti* poems themselves.

It is surprising, as in the first half of the century, that the vogue for Indian things barely carried into poetry. Hippie travelers in Rishikesh or Benares, the Beatles, Ravi Shankar, the invocation of Gandhi in the antiwar movement, Hare Krishnas in the airports, Ginsberg's harmonium and chanting at his countless readings, the popularity of yoga and the parade of mass-market gurus ... (Snyder, in a much-read essay in 1967, "Passage to More than India," had drawn a triangular *yantra* of Indian saddhus, Native Americans, and countercultural youth.) Yet there were only three noteworthy books of Indian lyric poetry by American poets, all slim: Denise Levertov's collaboration with Edward C. Dimock on Bengali songs, *In Praise of Krishna* (1967);

Robert Bly's *The Kabir Book* (1976), a rewriting of Tagore's translations; and W. S. Merwin's collaboration with J. Moussaieff Masson (later Jeffrey Masson of the Freud archive controversy), *Sanskrit Love Poetry* (1977, reprinted as *The Peacock's Egg*). A. K. Ramanujan, who lived much of his life in the US, had the Tamil poems of *The Interior Landscape* (1967) and one book that was popular among some poets: the Penguin *Speaking of Śiva* (1973), translations from the classical Kannada. Ramanujan was perhaps the closest to an Arthur Waley as both a literary figure and a scholar but, although revered in India, he was not widely known in the US. Among the Indologists, Barbara Stoler Miller, who died young, had a good translation of Bhartrihari (1967), and later of the *Gita*, and Daniel H. H. Ingalls's massive *An Anthology of Sanskrit Court Poetry* (1965) remains an inexhaustible delight. Among India-inspired American poems, the most memorable are Charles Olson's "Poem 143. The Festival Aspect" in the third volume of *The Maximus Poems* (written in 1965), which came out of his reading of Heinrich Zimmer's *Myths and Symbols in Indian Art and Civilization*, and—with Snyder, perhaps the greatest example of an American *bhakti* of transcendent erotic lyrics—Kenneth Rexroth's *The Love Poems of Marichiko* (1978), which however purports to be a translation of a contemporary Japanese woman poet.

Since then, the landscape has grown even sparser: some translations by the Indian poets Dilip Chitre, Arun Kolatkar, and especially Arvind Krishna Mehrotra; versions of Mirabai by Robert Bly and Jane Hirshfield, a few scholars (most notably David Shulman, an immensely prolific translator of classical Tamil and Telugu). The Kashmiri poet Aga Shahid Ali, was a great promoter of the Urdu *ghazal* form, but only he was able to bring it successfully to English. Andrew Schelling, is the first American poet to translate directly from the Sanskrit, but for some thirty years he has been virtually alone in the field.

Classical Indian poetry, with its millennia of texts, its many languages, its oceanic vastness, remains the largest blank on the West-

ern map of world literature. But beyond literary history, beyond the
many pleasures of the individual poems, it could serve the function of
translation at its best—that is, as inspiration. Here are ways of writing
poetry that do not exist in our language, but, transformed, could.

The arrival of the Spaniards in Mexico has often been compared to
the appearance of extraterrestrials (more exactly, extraterrestrials
before the age of science fiction, before we began to imagine what
they might be like). The bearded white men with their horses and
guns corresponded to nothing in the Mexican worldview; and, most
disastrously, the auto-immune systems of Mexican bodies had no experience with Spanish microbes. It has rarely been said, however, that
this was also an encounter of mutually incomprehensible poetics. (If
the conquistadors were largely illiterate soldiers, some of those who
followed them, particularly a few of the priests, had both education
and curiosity.)

Spain in the 16th century was writing traditional ballads and ro-
mances, and odes and elegies and ecologues inspired by the Latin. The
sonnet, newly imported from Italy, was the rage. Mexico in the 16th
century—to speak of only one of its poetries, the Aztec—had eleven
subgenres of lyric poetry that remain known to us: eagle songs, oce-
lot songs, spring songs, flower songs, war songs, divine songs, songs
of orphanhood (also known as "philosophical reflections"), tickling
songs , and songs of pleasure. The great religious Spanish poets of
the period, Fray Luís de León and San Juan de la Cruz (St. John of the
Cross) were humans who wrote in praise of God. The great religious
Aztec poetry—preserved in the *Cantares Mexicanos*—came as gifts directly from the gods to humankind. More astonishingly, it is believed
that the poems were themselves a kind of god, venerated ancestors
summoned to earth by the supplications of the poets.

The Aztec figurative system famously yoked two elements to form
an unexpected third: cacao was "heart and blood," misery was "stone
and wood," fame was "mist and smoke," pleasure "heat and wind."

(This tradition of conjunctions, seen through the eyes of Surrealism, would be reinvigorated, four hundred years later, by Octavio Paz.) A person could be a feather, jade, a cypress, a flute, a gold necklace, a city. Fray Diego Durán, one of the first priests who was interested, unironically said that their poems are "so obscure that there is no one who really understands them—except themselves alone."

Spanish poetry "conquered" Mexican poetry in the centers of culture, with the unforeseen consequence that the greatest Spanish-language poet of the second half of the 17th century (and indeed for two hundred years after that) was a Mexican: Sor Juana Inés de la Cruz. But poetry composed in the scores of native Mexican languages continued in the countryside, along with traditional customs, beliefs, and ways of making art. Most of this poetry was, of course, orally transmitted, and was unknown outside of its communities until anthropologists and others began transcribing and translating the poems in the 20th century. It is a poetry without literary history, in the sense that it arrives to us late in the story and we do not know how it evolved over the centuries—as though the earliest known English-language poet was William Carlos Williams. And it is a poetry without criticism, in that we rarely know its poetics or its standards—the details of its composition, or what its listeners considered to be good or bad.

In recent decades, there has been an extraordinary new development in Mexico's indigenous literatures. Bilingual writers, educated in Spanish and conversant in Western modernism, are choosing to write in their native languages. As these are contemporary writers, their poetry and fiction is disseminated orally not only in live performance but also on radio shows, and, for the first time in these histories, in books and language-specific magazines. Some of the poets use their native language as a way of enriching the modernist lyric; others use modernism to reimagine traditional forms.

What is happening in Mexico is being mirrored in certain other countries where indigenous languages survive. It is partially a matter of ethnic pride: In the globalizing world, there is a countercurrent that is emphasizing the local, celebrating what is different in the face of the monoculture, adapting the old ways in an era of relentless novelty. But it is also a culmination of modernism itself, the rallying cry of which was Joyce's "Here Comes Everybody." Twentieth-century painting and sculpture are inextricable from its discovery of new forms in African and Native American art; the stories, poems, and myths of tribal cultures permeate modern literature. (For some decades there was, in France, a very blurred line between Surrealist and anthropologist.) Yet this was, in the last century, all one-directional: the indigenous feeding the cosmopolitan West. We are now at a moment—still in its early stages—where inspiration is flowing the other way. The poetry written in Spanish and English and French is one part of a complex of ideas and perceptions that is invigorating new ways of writing in Mazatec, Zapotec, Xoque, Nahuatl, and other languages, which may in turn lead to something else, somewhere else.

Béla Balázs's Chinese Dreams

In the first decades of the 20th century, a committed modernist had two ambitions: to make something new and to recover something old. In the search for new forms for the new age, it seemed as though everything was inspirational, and that the entirety of human history was rushing into the present: the folk songs and folk tales of European peasants, African or Inuit masks, Japanese haiku, Celtic rituals, Navajo blankets, Etruscan funerary sculpture, the unreconstructed fragments of classical Greek poetry, Oceanic shields and tapa cloths, alchemical drawings . . . The way into the future and out of the recent past—the perceived straitjacket of 19th-century art and mores—was to go back to the distant past. (And, in the prevailing evolutionary narrative of culture, contemporary tribal art was seen as relics from the past, the "childhood of man.")

China, as the oldest continuing civilization, was inevitably magnetic. Paul Claudel was the vice-consul in Shanghai and Fuzhou, and modernist Sinophilia begins exactly in 1900 with his, perhaps overly Catholic, book of prose poetry, *Conaissance de l'est* (Knowledge of the East). He was followed by Victor Segalen, who went to China as a medical officer, produced a scholarly history of the stone statuary, and wrote two of the greatest books of chinoiserie: *Stèles*—prose-poem "translations" of nonexistent originals, based on stone inscription tablets, and published as a Chinese-style book in Bedang in 1912— and the uncharacterizable novel *René Leys*, set in the Forbidden City during the Boxer Rebellion, which appeared posthumously in 1922. Two years later, Saint-John Perse, who had served as secretary in the French embassy in Beijing, published *Anabasis*, a series of prose poems set in an imaginary Central Asia. Although somewhat forgotten now, it was, along with *The Waste Land*, the most internationally influential book of poetry of its time, and was translated by T. S. Eliot, Walter Benjamin, and Giuseppe Ungaretti. *Anabasis*, in turn led to Henri Michaux's 1932 *A Barbarian in Asia* (which was translated by Borges) and Michaux's lifelong experiments in a calligraphy attached to no language.

Nearly everywhere, ancient China was inextricable from the early avant-garde. The Mexican poet José Juan Tablada introduced Apollinaire's calligraphy-inspired concrete poems *(calligrammes)* into Spanish in 1920 with a book called *Li Po and Other Poems;* one of the poems is in the shape of the character for "longevity," a Taoist charm. The first major book in English of the new, imagistic, free verse was Ezra Pound's translations of largely Tang Dynasty poems, *Cathay*. Published in 1915, its poems from a thousand years earlier of soldiers, ruined cities, abandoned wives and friends, had an immediacy for those in the trenches and those waiting at home. And Pound discovered (or more exactly, semi-invented) in the structure of the Chinese ideogram itself a model for bringing disparate elements together into a single dynamic object of art. Sergei Eisenstein, studying Chinese, independently discovered the same thing, which he turned into his theory of film montage.

The modern German novel begins in 1915 with Alfred Döblin's *The Three Leaps of Wang Lun*, a remarkably well-researched historical novel, set in the 18th century, but written in the expressionistic style that Döblin perfected years later in *Berlin Alexanderplatz*. Gunter Grass has said that his own prose is "inconceivable without it." Bertolt Brecht loved the book, and it was perhaps the germ of his Sinophilia, which led to his translations of Arthur Waley's translations of Chinese poems; an adaptation of Li Xingdao's 13th-century play, *The Chalk Circle*, relocated to the Caucasus; and *The Good Person of Sichuan*. (Brecht, in turn, was the first contemporary Western dramatist to have his work presented in China.) At his death he left an unfinished play, *The Life of Confucius*, that was to be performed entirely by children.

It is probable that Brecht read Béla Balázs's 1922 contribution to

German Chinoiserie, *The Cloak of Dreams* (recently published in a new translation by Jack Zipes). What is certain is that they knew each other in the various theatrical and political circles in Berlin, and not happily: Brecht sued the director G. W. Pabst after he was fired—and Balázs hired—as the screenplay writer for the film version of Brecht's own *Threepenny Opera*.

Except among a few film and music scholars, Balázs is barely remembered, and only four books from the mountain of his works—novels, stories, poetry, plays, puppet plays, screenplays, libretti, and political articles—have ever been translated into English, all of them collections of his film criticism. But he was an archetypal modernist, a type that is now nearly extinct: the man who seemed to know everyone, do everything, and write everything.

Born Herbert Bauer in Szeged, Hungary, in 1884, he took the pseudonym Béla Balázs for the poems he was contributing to the local newspaper while still a schoolboy. At the university in Budapest, his roommate was Zoltán Kodály and his friends were Béla Bartók and György Lukács. With the two composers, he used to tour the countryside, collecting folk songs and fairy tales. After studies with Georg Simmel in Berlin and Henri Bergson in Paris, he returned to Budapest, where, among many other things, he wrote the libretto for Bartók's 1911 opera *Duke Bluebeard's Castle* and the story for the 1917 ballet *The Wooden Prince*—the only Balázs works that are still widely known.

A volunteer soldier in World War I, he became seriously ill and was luckily discharged early. He spent the rest of the war in Budapest as an antiwar polemicist and a participant in Lukács's Sunday Circle of radical intellectuals. An active supporter of the revolution that very briefly brought communism to Hungary in 1919, he was in charge of literary affairs for the new government, promoting theater and films and creating a department of folk tales. After the regime was overthrown by the neighboring Romanians and Czechs, Balázs, who had fought with the Red Army, escaped into exile in Vienna. Friends with

Robert Musil and Arthur Schnitzler, among other Viennese writers, he was also part of a crowd of Hungarian film exiles, including Sándor Kellner (who became Sir Alexander Korda), Mihály Kertész (who became Michael Curtiz), and Béla Lugosi (whose exotic roles no doubt allowed him to keep his name in Hollywood). He became the world's first film critic of note, inventing the idea of the daily film review for the newspaper *Der Tag*. His first book of film theory, *The Visible Man* (1924), was translated into eleven languages and was enormously influential among young directors, particularly in Germany and the Soviet Union, with its evocation of film's ability to speak a universal language of the body and its celebration of techniques previously impossible in the theatrical arts: the close-up and the point of view. "I do not watch Romeo and Juliet from the pit," he later wrote, "I look up to the balcony with Romeo's eyes and down at Romeo with Juliet's eyes. . . . I look at the world from their point of view and have none of my own. . . . Nothing like this kind of identification . . . has ever occurred in any other art." The distance between spectator and spectacle had been erased, much like the Chinese story he cites—also one of Walter Benjamin's favorites—of the painter who walks into his own painting.

In 1924, when radio broadcasts were just beginning—the one in Austria was less than a year old—Balázs imagined the birth of a new art form, the radio play, a theater strictly for the ears, as the silent cinema was strictly for the eyes. But, much like critics of the internet today, he warned that, with the whole world immediately accessible, radio would lead to a global homogenization of culture. Worse, radio would become a chaos of disembodied voices spreading both truths and falsehoods, where "the Communist can pose as a Fascist and the Fascist as a Communist," where "everyone can hear everything and no one knows what to believe."

He moved to Berlin in 1926, wrote and directed plays for Marxist theater collectives, collaborated with Erwin Piscator on agit-prop, and wrote a libretto for Ernst Krenek, as well as novels, stories, and hundreds of articles for newspapers and left-wing journals. He was a hot screenwriter, working with Pabst on *The Threepenny Opera*, Eisenstein on *The General Line*, and films by Kurt Bernhardt (who became Curtis Bernhardt) and Hermann Kosterlitz (who became Henry Koster). His box-office smash, Korda's *Madame Wants No Children* was an unlikely pro-abortion comedy, and featured a walk-on by the beautiful Marie Magdalene von Losch (who became Marlene Dietrich). A guru to the young Billy Wilder, his ideas would resurface in Walter Benjamin (who found him irritating in person, mystical and banal), Rudolf Arnheim, and Siegfried Kracauer. In 1930, his second book of film theory, *The Spirit of the Film*, was almost unique among cinephiles in welcoming the advent of talking pictures, and it presciently argued for the immediate establishment of film archives.

A popular German actress, Leni Riefenstahl, asked him to write the script for her first directorial effort, *The Blue Light*, an ethereal tale of a light in the mountains that appears with the full moon, luring young men to their deaths, and the beautiful young peasant woman who knows its secret source in a cave of blue crystals. Balázs was close to Riefenstahl on the set, and reportedly directed the scenes in which she appeared. He invited her to go with him to Moscow, where he had been hired to write a screenplay, but she had to stay and edit the film. By the time he returned, she had been born-again after a reading of *Mein Kampf*. She took his name off the credits of the film, refused to pay him, and referred to him, in a letter to Julius Streicher of *Der Stürmer*, as "the Jew Bela Balacs [*sic*]."

In 1933, National Socialism drove him permanently to the Soviet Union, where he taught and wrote plays, poems, and screenplays for the next, extremely difficult, fourteen years. Although he was under continual attack for such things as "subjective idealism," he managed, unlike many of the Hungarian Communists, to avoid execution or the gulag. How he managed remains unclear, and may have been pure chance. Much of the time he was living in the forest in a dacha far from Moscow, and there is speculation that he was simply forgotten.

During the war, he was in Kazakhstan, collecting folk tales, having unwisely turned down an offer to join the European exiles teaching at the New School in New York.

In 1947, he was sent back to the now Soviet-controlled Hungary, publishing a third book of film criticism, *Theory of the Film*, writing poems, novels, plays, articles, and collaborating on two films that had success abroad: Géza von Radványi's *Somewhere in Europe* (praised by André Bazin as a masterpiece of neo-realism) and István Stöts's *Song of the Cornfields*. Well-known in foreign film circles, he was inevitably denounced for "agitative secularism" and the like by the party orthodoxy at home—including his old friend Lukács, whom he helped to release from the Lubyanka prison during the war. He died in 1949, on the verge of moving to East Berlin as an adviser to the GDR film industry. Almost needless to say, he was posthumously honored by those who had attacked him, and the Béla Balázs Studio was founded in Budapest in 1959 to encourage young filmmakers.

Balázs wrote fairy tales his whole life, but *The Cloak of Dreams* was an unusual commissioned project. In 1921, the illustrator Mariette Lydis created a series of aquarelles on "Chinese" themes, in the style of a simplified Aubrey Beardsley, with some touches of German Expressionism. She then asked Balázs, in effect, to embody her illustrations by writing accompanying texts. He had three weeks to complete the project, as the publisher was eager to have it available for Christmas.

It is a tribute to Balázs's skills as a storyteller that he was able so quickly to spin elaborate tales out of single, simple scenes. The image of an obese mother suckling a baby turns into the story of a man who is thousands of years old because, for complicated reasons, he had to keep repeating his infancy. An equally obese couple sleeping becomes the story of a man who is reborn as a flea; he conspires with a talking silver fox to bring his future parents together so that he'll be reborn as a human. A straightforward portrait of a parasol-vendor leads Balázs to imagine an unhappily married street-peddler who finally finds peace at home after buying a series of magic parasols, each one of which produces a different kind of weather.

Despite the usual trappings of opium, jade, rice paper, bamboo, and tea, the stories, as might be expected, are not terribly Chinese. Most of them could easily have taken place in another exotic empire, Persia or India. They are much more in the tradition of the German Romantic *Kunstmärchen*, the literary fairy tales of the brothers Grimm or E. T. A. Hoffmann, or the contemporary Orientalist fairy tales that were being written by Hermann Hesse and Thomas Mann, than the Chinese rough equivalent, the "strange stories," best known in the West in Pu Songling's 17th-century *Strange Stories from a Chinese Studio*.

Chinese "strange stories" are more deadpan and satirical and, moreover, are meant to be reports of true events. A typical story is the man obsessed with peonies who forsakes his family and goes into debt when, in the middle of winter, he starts waiting for the peonies to blossom. Or the collector of rare breeds of pigeons who ceremoniously presents his best pair of specimens to a high-ranking official, who later tells him that they were indeed tasty, but not particularly different from ordinary pigeons. The stories are full of ghosts and demons. A man will marry a beautiful maiden, living happily with her until the day he discovers a demon with a pile of human skin, carefully applying makeup to it. Then the man must decide whether to keep on living in bliss with a monster.

The translator Jack Zipes claims that Balázs's tales were heavily influenced by Taoism, but this seems somewhat far-fetched and ignores the more likely Theosophism to which he was attracted. Despite the presence of an utterly idiosyncratic Laozi in one of the stories, Freud more often appears to be the resident sage: The skulls of a man's father, grandfather, and great-grandfather torment and eventually devour him. In the title story, the wife of the emperor weaves scenes from her dreams into her husband's cloak. She only desires him when he is wearing it; when he takes it off, her desire vanishes.

In the final story, a warrior must fight to win the hand of one of three princesses. He chops off the arm of the first suitor, but the eldest daughter takes pity and marries the wounded man; he chops off the leg of the second, but the middle daughter also takes pity and does the same; so he chops off the head of the third. The youngest daughter says that the poor man should not die without a widow to mourn him; the warrior, in a shockingly abrupt ending to the book, goes home and kills himself. And there are three stories of friendship that are said to reflect Balázs's contentious relationship with Lukács: feuding neighbors are reborn as Siamese twins; two inseparable friends turn into each other in a permanent opium dream; and—illustrating a grotesque picture of a fat man caning the naked buttocks of another—a man must beat his friend almost to death in order to save him.

The most Chinese (and simultaneously most modern) of Balázs's stories is one that was not part of the original collection: "The Book of Wan Hu-Chen." A penniless man is in love with the governor's daughter. She rebuffs him, so he decides to write a book about her, making her even more beautiful and elegant than she is in life. Eventually she comes out of the book to visit him, but Wan has made, out of modesty, a terrible authorial mistake. In the book she is in love with the dashing Prince Wang. Wan then has to write a chapter killing off Prince Wang. The maiden turns to Wan for solace, and they live on happily for many years—he, writing the book all day, giving her ever finer jewels and clothes; she, coming out of the book at night. But he grows older and poorer, having no other occupation, and she remains young and beautiful. They have a son who remains in the real world, and is the reincarnation of Prince Wang. Wan, penniless, finally gives the boy to the governor's family, discovers that the real daughter had died the day he began writing, and goes off into the pages of his own book to live in eternal springtime with his true love.

A somewhat similar Chinese "strange story" is more disturbing. A young man spends all of his time reading, but he's not very bright and cannot understand what he reads. He reads indiscriminately, day and night, in the enormous library he has inherited, never knowing the difference between a good book and a bad, a friendless, ridiculous figure who cannot pass his exams. He develops a longing for a woman he comes across in the pages of the *History of the Han Dynasty*. She, too, eventually comes out of the book to teach him, at age thirty-three, all the joys of life that eluded him while he was reading. He has never known such ecstasy. But then a local magistrate, hearing rumors of a demon in the house, burns down the library. Devastated, the bookworm's obsession turns into a dedication to revenge. He quickly passes his exams, becomes the governor, and ultimately destroys his enemy, though he has, of course, forever lost the maiden.

The fairy tale, in the first decades of the 20th century, served various contradictory agendas. It was the voice of the People, uncorrupted by bourgeois values; or it was the expression of a national spirit, of a Folk unpolluted by foreign influence; or it was the manifestation of universal psychological states, the tropes of a collective unconscious.

For Balázs, the good modernist, what was thrilling was the connection between films and fairy tales, what was newest and what was most archaic. The previously unseen worlds presented in nature films were like fairyland; the entirely self-contained universe of cartoons was like fairyland; Charlie Chaplin was like the fairy tale of the ignorant farmer who thought he could carry sunlight into a windowless church in his sack. "For the urban population of today," he wrote in 1922, "the cinema is what folk songs and folktales used to be." Robert Musil said that reading Balázs on film was like reading the anthropologist Lucien Lévy-Bruhl on magical thinking.

Unlike others, he did not believe that the movies would mean the end of stories and novels, and it is not surprising that he wrote *The Cloak of Dreams* at the same time that he wrote his first screenplay. In the present moment, when fiction has yet again been declared dead, these deliberately anachronistic, pseudo-Oriental, and completely delightful tales are further examples of the perennial human need for imaginative narrative told in words.

In Yorkshire, where Herbert Read was born in 1893 on a remote farm at the western end of the Vale of Pickering, south of the moors and north of the wolds, young girls would pin ivy leaves together and throw them into wishing wells, and supernatural hares could only be killed with pellets of pure silver. Two sisters, nuns in the convent of Beverley, vanished into the moonlight on Christmas Eve and were found asleep at the convent door in May. A white horse would appear, hovering over the river, on the day someone would drown, and at night the bargest, the spectral hound, dragged its large and clanking chain. The images of two veiled women in white and a small child would flit from window to window in the Trinity Church, and the bells en route to St Hilda's abbey, lost in a shipwreck, could still be heard from under the waters. There, the hapless cowherd Caedmon was instructed in a dream how to sing the origin of things and the dying William the Hermit performed his own burial; seven witches, in the shape of black cats and crows, possessed the daughters of Edward Fairfax, the translator of Tasso. It was said that a village—no one remembered its name—suddenly sank under a lake because it had refused hospitality to a poor beggar. The rivers were inhabited by kelpies, who claimed one human victim every year, and fairies played in Craven Dales among the Druid rocks of Almas Cliffe and the ancient burial mounds of Willy Houe.

At the age of ten, following the accidental death of his father, Read was torn from his enchanted pastorale and sent to the city of Halifax and the regimented hell of the Crossley & Porter Orphan Home & School, its walls black from the smoke of the surrounding factories. From the orphanage he moved into the vaster industrial desolation of Leeds to attend the university, and from there into the trenches of the First World War, where he was a decorated hero who carried a copy of *Walden* in his rucksack. Innocence and experience became lifelong themes in his work.

Masked by reticence and cloaked in tweeds, Read was the unexpectedly ardent and frighteningly prolific champion of nearly everything that was radical in the first half of the 20th century: Imagism, Surrealism, abstraction, the Bauhaus, Marxism, anarchism, Freud and Jung, progressive education, Gandhian nonviolent resistance. Though now somewhat dimly remembered, he was, for decades, the Victoria Station of the arts, England's primary explainer of the modern.

The Meaning of Art; Art Now; Art and Industry; Art and Society; The Philosophy of Modern Art; Art and the Evolution of Man; A Concise History of Modern Painting; A Concise History of Modern Sculpture; to name only a few ... A curator of ceramics at the Victoria and Albert Museum, author of monographs on stained glass and Staffordshire pottery, he became in the 1930s the leading exponent of the new British art (Henry Moore, Ben Nicholson, Barbara Hepworth, Paul Nash, Naum Gabo), most of them his neighbors in a colony in Hampstead, and ultimately wrote books on each of them. His predilection was for the new abstraction, but he was equally enthusiastic for abstraction's sworn enemy and mischievous twin: Surrealism. He organized, with Roland Penrose, the famous Surrealist exhibition of 1936, where Dalí lectured wearing a diving helmet, Dylan Thomas served boiled string in a teacup, the press went wild over Madame Breton's green fingernails, and T. S. Eliot obsessed over Meret Oppenheim's fur-lined teacup as, in the words of the painter Eileen Agar, the "super-objective correlative of the female sex." Read opened the proceedings with the words, "Do not judge this movement kindly. It is defiant—the desperate act of men too profoundly convinced of the rottenness of our civilization to want to save a shred of respectability." But it was said that he was mortified at a party when the fabulous Lee Miller danced naked around him.

Inspired by the Bauhaus and the first years of the Soviet Union, he believed that a new society required a revolution in industrial design. He founded the Design Research Unit, a kind of informal academy of design, whose most unlikely project was a Jowett car designed by Gabo. His own minimalist flat in Hampstead was furnished with pieces by Alvar Aalto and Mies van der Rohe, and the 1933 *Art Now* was among the first books printed entirely in sans-serif type. The following year, *Art and Industry*, designed by Herbert Bayer of the Bauhaus with photos selected by Moholy-Nagy, was itself both a description and an icon of the new design.

In the 1940s, he founded the Institute of Contemporary Art, Britain's first museum space for the modern, while devoting much of his time to the idea that education could be transformed by emphasizing the creative arts. *Education Through Art* in 1943 was his best-selling book, and possibly most influential on the society at large: a manifesto that led to reimagined curricula in the traditional schools and the founding of experimental schools both for children and artists. Curator, juror, gallerist, publicist, columnist: when a new generation of art critics rose in revolt in the 1950s, Read was their primary target. As Lawrence Alloway explained, "There was nobody much else to attack . . . Herbert was really all there was."

Phases of English Poetry; Form in Modern Poetry; In Defense of Shelley; Wordsworth; The True Voice of Feeling; Poetry and Experience; to name a few . . . Read's campaign as a literary and art critic was a reconciliation of—or at least equal enthusiasm for—warring camps, declaring them both essential to the modern. On the one side, the "geometric": the ahistorical beauty of abstract art and the literary classicism promoted by his lifelong friend T. S. Eliot, I. A. Richards, and the New Critics. On the other, the "organic": the personal, "vital" art represented by the English Romantics (who were dismissed by Pound and Eliot) and the new Surrealism. A Freudian, and later an even more committed Jungian, he was the first English critic to apply both versions of psychoanalytic theory to literature and the arts, was the general editor of Jung's collected writings in the great Bollingen edition and a regular at the Eranos conferences. As an editor at Routledge, he introduced Samuel Beckett's *Murphy* (which had been rejected by forty-two publishers), Simone Weil, and Martin Buber, among many others, and was responsible for the Bollingen editions of Coleridge and Valéry.

The Philosophy of Anarchism; The Education of Free Men; Anarchy and Order; To Hell With Culture; Freedom: Is It a Crime?; The Politics of the Unpolitical; Existentialism, Marxism and Anarchism, to name a few . . . Read converted from Marxism to anarchism during the Spanish Civil War, worked closely with Emma Goldman during her London years, edited an anthology of Kropotkin's writings, and was a leading light in the various anarchist groups, from the Freedom Press to the Committee of 100. He loathed Churchill, and dreamed that the ruins of the Blitz would lead to the building of an entirely new, socially just, community-based society. As the years went by, Gandhi remained the only political leader he admired and his pacifism hardened into an absolute, leading him to condemn even groups whose aims he otherwise supported, such as the Hungarian resistance and the anti-nuclear bomb demonstrators. His letters and writings on the corruption of capitalism, the oppression of communism, and the ugliness, soullessness, and environmental degradation of modern life were increasingly strident. Spending most of his time in cities, he detested cities.

In 1953, his surprising decision to accept a knighthood led to ridicule and ostracism from the anarchist and leftist ranks, but no wavering in his beliefs. Visiting communes in China in 1959, Sir Herbert mistook them for Kropotkin's complete decentralization of industry; visiting an American supermarket, he thought it would be the model of Kropotkin's anarchist distribution of goods, if only the cash registers were removed. Of Americans he observed:

> One of the most curious characteristics of this people is their complete misunderstanding of democracy. They do not believe

in *equality*, but in "equality of *opportunity*." They confess that again & again, with pride, without realizing that "equality of opportunity" is merely the law of the jungle, that they are not egalitarians, but opportunists . . .

In 1949, he moved back to Yorkshire, a few miles from his childhood home. He wrote: "In spite of my intellectual pretensions, I am by birth and tradition a peasant. I remain essentially a peasant. . . . The only class in the community for which I feel any real sympathy is the agricultural class . . . " Yet he was in London as often as he could, and his seemingly far-fetched peasantness was quite real in the English caste system: Edith Sitwell, who plagiarized him, found him a "crashing bore." Virginia Woolf thought he looked like a "shop assistant." Entering Read's house for the first time, she asked loudly, "Is this a stable?" At a dinner for Read and his wife's relatives, Eliot, though he admired Read's mind, fed them chocolates made of soap.

He died from cancer in 1968; his gravestone reads "KNIGHT, POET, ANARCHIST," two of which seem like odd choices from the possible list of accomplishments. He did indeed write poetry throughout his life, but most of the poems tend toward vagueness and imitation; they had few enthusiasts. Richard Aldington told him that he was writing too much criticism to be a poet; T. E. Lawrence told him to stop complaining that he was writing too much criticism. Stephen Spender, in a review, was nastier: "There is a romantic side of Mr. Read's nature which seems to believe that, given slightly different circumstances, entirely different and much better poems and books would have emerged from his study, like rabbits from a hat." Eliot only recognized him as a critic. Pound liked him personally, but found his poetry "bloody dull."

In financial straits for most of his life, he wrote, every week, book reviews, film reviews, art reviews, and reviews of mystery novels, and was on a neverending loop of lecture tours, committee meetings, and social functions. Graham Greene was the godfather of his daughter.

J. R. Ackerley stored scandalous letters from E. M. Forster in his safe. Eliot, with whom he lunched fortnightly, sang "Frankie and Johnny" at a party in his Hampstead house. The teenaged Denise Levertov used to invent excuses to come over to stare at his paintings and books. Just before the Second World War, George Orwell wanted the two of them to buy a printing press in order to publish anti-government pamphlets under the inevitable censorship. Stravinsky was a friend, and Picasso, and Man Ray, and Dag Hammarskjöld, and nearly everyone else on the peaks of Western civilization. His unlikely friendship with the maniacally bitter Edward Dahlberg—who said that Ford Madox Ford and Read were the only "men of letters" who defended him—led to an odd book of epistolary exchanges on modern writers, *Truth Is More Sacred*, with Dahlberg, at his most hyperbolic, doing most of the writing. In Havana, at a Cultural Congress a few months before he died, weak from radiation therapy, Read was met with silence when he declared: "I shall say only one sentence. The revolutionary ideal of the 19th century was internationalist; in the 20th century it became enclosed in nationalism and the only internationalists left are the artists."

Ford Madox Ford had told Read, in 1920, to get out of cultural journalism and become a novelist: "You may not like novel writing but it would be a good thing to stick to it as to avoid turning your soul into a squirrel in a revolving cage." Though he had often imagined himself as a novelist in the manner of Henry James or his friend Edith Wharton, it was not until the summer of 1934 that he spent six weeks in a tiny, six-by-four-foot wooden hut he had built in his garden, writing his one, short novel.

> It was queer how the book wrote itself; I had nothing much to invent—only the local color. The details of the myth were waiting in my mind. And it was only afterwards that I began to see their significance.

It was originally called *Inland Far*, from Wordsworth's "Intimations of Immortality" ("Though inland far we be, / Our Souls have sight of that immortal sea / Which brought us hither.") Luckily this was quickly changed to *The Green Child*. (The abstraction Read favored in the visual arts often had a way of undermining his own writing, particularly in the poetry.) The surviving manuscript has a mysterious and completely misleading epigraph from Kierkegaard: "Reminiscence"—"Self" is crossed out, then "The power of reflection" is crossed out—"is the condition of all productivity."

Faber and Faber rejected the book; the editor Frank Morley writing Read—it's hard to believe this is Eliot's Faber—that it needed some "*some* belly . . . some drink somewhere, some honest fucking." Heinemann published it the next year at Richard Aldington's urging. New Directions brought out the American edition in 1948 and has kept it in print since—proving, perhaps, that it is the one book of Read's that will continue to be read. Graham Greene loved it and wrote an introduction to a later edition, though Read complained that it was too Catholic; Jung said that he couldn't sleep after reading it; Spender charged that Read was a mediocre writer because he had "no sense of evil." (A strange charge, as one of the characters, Kneeshaw, would seem to embody what later would be called the "banality of evil"). In the daily *New York Times*, Orville Prescott called it "ridiculous as well as vexatious"; a few days later, in the Sunday *Book Review*, Robert Gorham Davis (father of Lydia) found it "chilling," "beautifully imagined and beautifully written," but thought that it seemed "an emotional and symbolic reaction against everything that Read stands for intellectually."

It is a novel best read in complete ignorance of its contents. Even to know that it is full of surprises leads to the expectation of surprise. Many readers will be hooked in the first paragraph, the rest, most probably, on the thirteenth page. Scholars have found bits inspired by, or lifted from, Thomas Keightley's *The Fairy Mythology* (1833), W. H. Hudson's *Green Mansions* (Rima the bird girl) and his utopian novel *The Crystal Age*, John and William Robertson's *Letters on Paraguay* (1838–39), H. Rider Haggard's *Montezuma's Daughter*, and Benjamin Jowett's translation of Plato's *Phaedo* (1893). Perhaps he had also read O. Henry's one novel, *Cabbages and Kings*, which, though utterly different, opens with a similar plot device. In certain ways, just beyond the grasp of analysis, *The Green Child* belongs alongside two later short novels, set in villages, somewhat surrealist, inexplicably allegorical, and continually haunting: Juan Rulfo's *Pedro Paramo* and Tayeb Salih's *Season of Migration to the North*.

Late in his life, Read wrote:

> That I can combine anarchism with order, a philosophy of strife with pacifism, an orderly life with romanticism and revolt in art and literature—all this is inevitably scandalous to the conventional philosopher. This principle of flux, the Keatsian notion of "negative capability," justifies everything I have written, every attack and defense. I hate all monolithic systems, all logical categories, all pretenses to truth and inevitability. The sun is new every day.

At the end, he was still in the trenches, and still carrying a copy of Thoreau.

Aelian, in the 2nd century, said of the hyena fish—a creature no longer known to ichthyologists—that if you cut off its right fin and put it under your pillow, you will have terrifying visions. Edgar Cayce, a half-forgotten American psychic in the first half of the 20th century, claimed that he could put a book under his pillow and wake the next morning having totally absorbed its contents through osmosis. How many nights did Jeffrey Yang have to sleep with lobster claws, starfish arms, barnacles, the tentacles of squid and anemones, the tiny jaw of a parrotfish, and the curling tail of a seahorse under his pillow? And did he alternate them with copies of Rousseau and Pliny, Chuang Tzu and Sor Juana, George Oppen and the *Gita*, innumerable volumes of anthropology and history and natural history, bilingual dictionaries and newspaper clippings? Reading this *Aquarium* of unlikely, intense, and musically complex lyric poems, one is tempted to attribute its erudition to osmosis, its imagination to talismanic agents. It is a young poet's first book, but seems to be the product of a long life.

Despite the thousands of miles of coastlines and the long seafaring histories, marine life has been almost entirely absent from British and American poetry: the last memorable poems were written by D. H. Lawrence in the early 1920s. Matthew Arnold stands on Dover Beach, but he never wades into the water to discover its parallel universes. Walt Whitman and Charles Olson are forever gazing out to sea and occasionally actually go fishing, but they are more concerned with the human labor than the life of its objects. Thoreau is often deep below the surface of his self, but not that of Walden Pond. Emily Dickinson uses the word "fish" once, metaphorically; Marianne Moore has a few aquatic abstractions; Hugh MacDiarmid is more concerned with the geology than the biology of the sea. The greatest American novel is an allegorical encyclopedia of cetacean fact and lore, but in American poetry there is perhaps only one famous sea-creature: the sunfish given by the 19th-century naturalist Louis Agassiz to a student. Ezra Pound—who got it from a bogus guru, Yogi Ramacharaka, otherwise known as Bill Atkinson from Baltimore—tells the story at the opening of his *ABC of Reading* and many poets have repeated it: Agassiz asks the student to describe the fish and he produces a standard Linnaean taxonomy. Agassiz sends him back to the fish and he writes a four-page scientific essay. Agassiz tells him to go back and really look at the fish. "At the end of three weeks the fish was in an advanced state of decomposition, but the student knew something about it."

In the tripartite division of poetry into image, sound, and ideas, the beings who live in the sea would seem to belong to image alone. We watch them in fascination but—whales and dolphins aside— we cannot hear them. Traditionally, only a few—the mammals, the shark, the oyster with its pearl—have suggested any ideas at all. It is one of the marvels of Yang's *Aquarium* that these are not merely strange or pretty creatures flitting or floating by. Instead, he presents a whole history of human culture, seen from a submarine perspective: "Beneath / history is another history we've made / without *knowing* it." He rarely anthropomorphizes: he's neither Aesop nor a Grimm brother. But in the late modern obsession with reaching out toward the other, he has found the ultimate others—sponges, eels, abalones—who are us.

Unusually among American poets of his generation, with their tendency toward irony or standup performance or anecdotal memoir, Yang returns poetry to both its epic and lyric functions. Epic: as a storehouse of information, of what a culture knows about itself and the natural world, about the gods and about other humans. Lyric: as both celebration and excoriation, wonder at the world and rage at how it often is.

Moreover, lyric poetry—that little house where the absent lover lives—often serves as the same kind of wish-fulfillment that Freud attributed to dreams. In this era of the massive destruction of habitats, the extinction of species, and the depopulation of the oceans from pollution and industrial fishing, it is no surprise that a poet, however urban, should turn to a form of pastoral elegy—not in the meadows but under the waves. The lyric has always attempted to stop time; the great ones never age; to sing of the creatures that inhabit this book is to momentarily, however hopelessly, arrest their retreat, to keep them alive somewhere, if only in a book. There are hints throughout, but when we reach the "Z" of this abecedarium it is clear that beneath all the wit and erudition is a larger despair, as the perfect, eternal, self-perpetuating ecosystem of the coral reefs of the South Pacific enters human history as the symbol of the end of the earth.

Thoreau, reading Confucius by Walden Pond, notes a passage that describes the world as "an ocean of subtle intelligences." It is the world of *An Aquarium* and, in its way, is *An Aquarium* itself.

Charles Reznikoff's "Testimony"

Charles Reznikoff may be the most elusive poet in American poetry and his book-length *Testimony* the most elusive long poem of modernism. He is remembered as a kind of New York saint, an urban Emily Dickinson: the Unknown Poet, walking the city streets, writing intense, seemingly matter-of-fact lyrics of things he saw and heard. And then, in the last decades of his life, devoting himself to two obsessional projects of narrative vignettes: the more than five hundred pages of *Testimony*, drawn from turn-of-the-century American court cases, and the hundred pages of *Holocaust*, taken from the transcripts of the Nuremberg and Eichmann trials. Certainly the outlines of both the poet's life and the poems' processes are plain enough, but the rest tends to be filled in with negatives: all the things the poet did not do and all the things the poems aren't.

Reznikoff, born in New York in 1894, graduated NYU law school in 1916, passed the bar, but only briefly practiced, preferring to become a salesman for his father's hat business. (He said much later that law was too much work for a poet, whereas he could write his poems in the hours spent waiting in Macy's for the buyer to show up.) After that business collapsed, he held random jobs throughout his life: writer of entries for a legal encyclopedia, *Corpus Juris*; managing editor of *The Jewish Frontier*; editor of the papers of the lawyer and civil rights activist Louis Marshall; co-author of a history of the Jews of Charleston and an unfinished history of the Jews of Cleveland. His one extended stay outside of New York City—he never left the US—was the three years he spent in the 1930s in Hollywood as an assistant to his old friend, the producer Albert Lewin. Given a huge office at Paramount Pictures, he had little to do and wrote poems about watching the flies on his desk.

In the late 1920s he met two younger poets, Louis Zukofsky and George Oppen. The three, all Jewish New Yorkers, shared an admiration for Ezra Pound and William Carlos Williams and the belief, along with Williams, that American modernism should be relocated from Paris and London to the US. Asked to edit an issue of *Poetry* in 1931, Zukofsky put them together, along with Williams, Carl Rakosi, Basil Bunting, Kenneth Rexroth, and a stylistically random collection of others (including the young Whittaker Chambers), under the rubric of "Objectivists." His manifesto in the issue was called "Sincerity and Objectification: With Special Reference to the Work of Charles Reznikoff." (Typical of Reznikoff's fate and Zukofsky's personality, when the essay was reprinted decades later, Zukofsky omitted Reznikoff entirely.) In 1934, the three poets pooled their resources to create the Objectivist Press in order to publish themselves and Williams. The press didn't last long, but the label stuck, although the actual poetry of the three had little in common. Reznikoff may have been the only one to take the name seriously. Nearly forty years later, when asked to describe his poetry for the reference book *Contemporary Poets*, he wrote (in its entirety):

> "Objectivist"; images clear but the meaning not stated but suggested by the objective details and the music of the verse; words pithy and plain; without the artifice of regular meters; themes, chiefly Jewish, American, urban.

Until his mid-sixties, he published nearly all his books himself, setting the type for many of them on a printing press in his parents' basement. For eighteen of those years, there were no books of poetry at all. He received few reviews, most of them terrible. His first review said that he "annoys and bewilders"; his second called the poems "sordid, with an emphasis on the *sore*." The third, by Malcolm Cowley, said that he was "astigmatic," "an ecstatic with a defect in his voice, who stammers at the moment of greatest feeling." A line in Cowley's review—"He is unable to focus, and lines of splendid verse are lost to sight among heaps of rubbish"—may have led to one of Reznikoff's best-known short poems:

> Among the heaps of brick and plaster lies
> a girder, still itself among the rubbish.

It was a poem that Oppen often said ran through his mind over and over as he was trapped in a foxhole among dead and wounded comrades in the Second World War. Oppen, tellingly, always misquoted the last word as "rubble."

In 1962, New Directions, in collaboration with the *San Francisco Review* (run by Oppen's sister, June Degnan) published *By the Waters of Manhattan: Selected Verse*. Reznikoff's first visible book of poetry, it had an odd introduction by C. P. Snow, then famous as a social critic, who, "as far as a Gentile can judge," found the work had "overtones of extraordinary unfamiliarity." Three years later, the two publishers brought out the first volume of *Testimony*. In *Poetry*, Hayden Carruth—who had praised *By the Waters*—wrote: "I don't see the point in it." Surprisingly jingoistic, he claimed that the "material—all ugly, brutal, and inhumane . . . is one of relentless, absorbing, cold, bitter contempt: contempt for the society in question." Both books sold poorly; the ND-SFR collaboration ended; Reznikoff went back to printing his own books.

But in the 1960s the "Objectivists" emerged from their decades of near-total obscurity, like a council of Wise Elders suddenly among us. Oppen and Rakosi returned after their long silences; Zukofsky was published by major presses; Bunting in the UK produced his masterpiece, *Briggflatts*; in Wisconsin, the reclusive Lorine Niedecker was writing her best work. And Reznikoff was with them. There were readings, interviews, a prize or two. In 1974, the Black Sparrow Press began a program of bringing all of Reznikoff's poetry back into print. He died in 1976, at eighty-one, having just revised the proofs of a two-volume *Collected Poems*.

There was the legend of Charles Reznikoff, the invisible poet, walking twenty miles a day in New York City, writing down his observations in a little notebook, meeting cronies who never knew he was a writer at the Automat, publishing his own books of perfect poems for over fifty years. A sweet, elderly man who was maddeningly self-deprecating. George and Mary Oppen told me about a reading in Michigan, at the end of which the audience was on its feet, wildly cheering. Rezi, as they called him, was heard to mumble: "I hope I haven't taken up too much of your time."

And yet, because of his collaborations from the 1920s to the 1950s as editor and writer for such magazines as *The Menorah Journal* and *The Jewish Frontier*, he believed himself part of a milieu—if not exactly part of the crowd—of Upper West Side Jewish intellectuals. He had a very long marriage, though often spent apart, with Marie Syrkin, the dynamic journalist, academician, and Zionist activist; best friend of Golda Meir and a primary mentor to the young men who took over *The New Republic* in the 1970s. Reznikoff refused to accompany her on her many trips to postwar Europe, Palestine, and later Israel—explaining that he hadn't finished exploring Central Park—but happily went to the meetings and fundraising dinners, content, as he said many times, to sit at a table below while his wife sat on the dais. He was a frequent guest at the extravagant Hollywood and New York homes of the Lewins, where he is known to have dined with George Cukor, Nazimova, Djuna Barnes, and no doubt many others; he chatted with Greta Garbo on the street. He was perhaps most in his element at the Automat, but he also inhabited, however peripherally, Hollywood and Jewish high societies. Most of all, this kind, self-effacing man spent most of the last decades of his life in the systematic investigation of humanity at its worst: *Testimony* and *Holocaust*. It's too easy to call them the products of rage, inaccurate to attribute any politics or reflection on human nature to them. The fact is we will never know why these books were written, only how.

Testimony began as a book of prose in the 1930s, based on the 19th-century legal documents that Reznikoff was reading for *Corpus*

Juris and other historical documents. Probably inspired by Williams's *In the American Grain* (1925) and John Dos Passos's *Manhattan Transfer* in the same year and the first two volumes of his *U.S.A.* trilogy (1930 and 1932), it was written at a time when there was a preoccupation with telling the "American story" and the conviction that some kind of documentary narrative was the way to tell it. (Reznikoff's original title was *My Country 'Tis of Thee*, which was not necessarily ironic.) Given that it has only three sections—"Southerners and Slaves," "Sailing-Ships and Steamers," and "East and West"—it appears to be the beginning of a much larger panorama. Its most uncharacteristic piece, the prose poem "Rivers and Seas, Harbors and Ports," is an extraordinary reverie of the words and images of a vanished maritime world. It was unlike anything Reznikoff wrote before or after; a road not taken in his work:

> ... a cargo of sandalwood at the Fiji Islands and at Guam a quantity of beech de mer, betel nuts, and deer horns; ivory rings for martingales; a cargo of copper ore, shipped in Chile; sperm and whale oil, sperm candles and whalebone; pigs of copper; six seroons of indigo; pigs of lead, moys of salt, and frails of raisins; seal skins, prime fur and pup skins, from seals taken at the Falkland Islands; a cargo of tea, fresh, prime, and of the finest chop, quarter chests of tea, hyson skin and congo, with the present of a shawl from the hong merchant in Canton; cases, trunks, bales, casks, kegs, and bundles ...

The book was published in 1934 by the Objectivist Press with an introduction by Kenneth Burke, and has been scandalously out of print since. (The copy I own came from the library of William Carlos Williams; when I bought it, the pages were uncut.)

Sometime in the 1950s, he returned to *Testimony*, this time confining himself to legal cases of criminality and negligence and writing it as poetry. The project was divided into four chronological periods

(1885–1890, 1891–1900, 1901–1910, 1911–1915), in turn divided into three geographical areas (North, South, West), which contained subcategories—some critics have read them as serial poems—such as "Machine Age," "Domestic Scenes," "Property," "Railroads," "Negroes," "Sounds and Smells," "Social Life," "Children," and so on, most of which repeat throughout the book. As far as I know, no one has investigated the structure of the book in search of determining patterns.

His research for *Testimony* was almost unimaginable. The known source for merely one of the short poems is a court transcript that runs to a hundred pages. As Reznikoff said in an interview: "I might go through a volume of a thousand pages and find just one case from which to take the facts and rearrange them so as to be interesting. ... I don't know how many thousands of volumes I went through, and all I could manage to get out of it were these poems." (Characteristically, he adds: "And in looking through the book I might throw out some of them.") He frequently said that his original inspiration was, remarkably, Theodore Dreiser's *An American Tragedy* (1925—the same year as the Williams and Dos Passos books). But where Dreiser had expanded a single case into a massive novel, Reznikoff condensed massive documents into brief poems:

> It was nearly daylight when she gave birth to the child,
> lying on the quilt
> he had doubled up for her.
> He put the child on his left arm
> and took it out of the room,
> and she could hear the splashing of water.
> When he came back
> she asked him where the child was.
> He replied: "Out there—in the water."
> He punched up the fire
> and returned with an armload of wood
> and the child,

and put the dead child into the fire.
She said: "O John, don't!"
He did not reply
but turned to her and smiled.

These are notably crimes without punishment: We never learn how the judge or jury ruled in the case. The legal arguments are not represented. In some poems we have the scene of the crime without the crime itself. There is no commentary or rumination or metaphorical imagery; larger conclusions are not drawn. *Testimony*, as a cantata or mass, is a "Recitative"—the book's subtitle—with no chorales.

What Reznikoff liked about courtroom testimony, he said, was that what matters is the facts of the case, what the witness saw and heard, not the witness's feelings about, or interpretations of those facts. It was his ideal for poetry. He often cited some lines from the Sung Dynasty poet Wei T'ai (which he found in A.C. Graham's *Poems of the Late T'ang*): "Poetry presents the thing in order to convey the feeling. It should be precise about the thing and reticent about the feeling." His aim, in *Testimony*, was to create a "mood or feeling" by the "selection" and "arrangement" of the facts, as well as by the "rhythm of the words." (Despite Hayden Carruth's claim that "this is not poetry at all, but prose printed in irregular lines," the poems tend to have cleverly hidden internal rhymes and assonances.) Curiously, the closest thing to *Testimony* in literature—there are certainly no American poems remotely like it—may be the Icelandic sagas that Reznikoff loved: scenes of sheer human drama presented in the most unadorned of narratives:

The young man had been at work during the day
clearing land about their home:
it was a small, one-story log house
reached by a bypath from the road,
among some small jack pine and scrub oak brush.

The house was lighted by two small windows:
one on the north and one to the east.

His wife—a young woman of sixteen
who had been engaged to be married to a neighbor,
a man of sixty,
before she married Peter—
lighted the lamp
and spread a light meal on the table—
bread and milk. The meal over,
Peter took his accordion from the shelf
and sitting right opposite the window to the east
played "Home, Sweet Home."
He had just finished playing it
when a shot was fired from the outside.
Several buckshot pierced his head
and death was so sudden
he still sat upright in his chair
with the accordion in his hands.

Reznikoff is sometimes considered a precursor of the current
vogue for "appropriated" or "found" poetry—the copying of texts,
often of extreme banality, verbatim. He occasionally used a few
words or a bit of local speech from the courtroom transcripts, but
mainly what he "found" were the facts, which he then wrote in his
own way. The poems are not pastiches; the original manuscripts of
Testimony are covered with revisions. Reznikoff's personality bears
some resemblance to Bartleby, but he was no scrivener.

Testimony is indeed an American panorama: the cases come from
every state of the union and are full of things indigenous in north,
south, and west. The passion of the crimes is universal; the accounts
of racism (against "Negroes," Chinese, Mexicans) regional; the industrial accidents, derived from negligence lawsuits, are fixed in their

historical moment. Yet there is a classicism about it: Reznikoff considered himself a Hellenist, influenced by both the lyrics of the Greek Anthology and the tragic dramas. In *Testimony*, the machines are the gods, enacting their inexplicable acts of vengeance on the hapless humans, many of them children:

All revolving shafts are dangerous
but a vertical shaft,
neither boxed nor guarded against,
most dangerous.

The girl's work for the company was changed
to sweeping the floors:
among other places the floor of a room
where the shaft in a passageway—
between the wall and a machine—
ran from the floor to the ceiling.
In sweeping around it one morning
her apron was caught
and drawn about the shaft
and she was whirled around
striking the wall and machinery.

In the poems, the machines are usually described in detail, but the people are often nameless and nearly always featureless. They are merely actors in some unportrayed greater drama at the moment when their particular fates are sealed. And in these testimonies without judgments, their fates belong to perhaps the deepest substratum of this obsessional project: the Jewish narrative of suffering without redemption, epitomized, of course, by the Book of Job. From *Testimony*, Reznikoff would go on, near the end of his life, to the transcripts of the Nuremberg and Eichmann trials to create an even more devastating book, *Holocaust*, which recounts scenes from the Final Solution without comment and without the rhetoric of outrage:

They gathered some twenty *Hasidic* Jews from their homes,
in the robes these wear,
wearing their prayer shawls, too,
and holding prayer books in their hands.
They were led up a hill.
Here they were told to chant their prayers
and raise their hands for help to God
and, as they did so,
the officers poured kerosene under them
and set it on fire.

The twenty-five-year-old Lionel Trilling, who probably met Reznikoff through his college friend Zukofsky, reviewing Reznikoff's one commercial publication—the 1930 novel of a Jewish immigrant, also called *By the Waters of Manhattan*—wrote: "It has a quality of privacy which is startling. It has been written by a mind that, at once shy and unabashed, stays with itself, and, unintimidated by stale ways of seeing, makes public objects fresh in the freshness of its privacy." Reznikoff had a lifelong preoccupation with Jewish history and themes, but almost never attended a synagogue. He spent decades investigating crimes of social injustice, but expressed no political beliefs. He read very little contemporary American poetry, preferring the poets of the Greek Anthology or classical China. He once said, of something he had seen in a magazine: "When I read a poem like this, I turn the page."

Bibliography

(The Cloud Bookcase)

Absorption of Solar and Lunar Essences
by Anonymous (4th century)

Alchemy of the Purple Coil
by Anonymous (12th century)
 A treatise on sexuality. The female sexual organ is referred to as
 the "furnace of the reclining moon." A later commentator notes
 that "it has never been known that one can obtain immortality by
 mounting women."

Arcane Essay on the Supreme Cultivation of True Nature
by Anonymous (14th century)
 Recommends the avoidance of sleep.

Arcane Notes on the Cultivation of True Nature
by Fu Tu-jen (11th century)
 Dietary instructions. In the seventh and eighth months, worms
 should be eaten.

Biographies of Presumed Immortals
by Anonymous (10th century)

*Biography of Mr. Yang, Imperial Chamberlain, Senior Assistant of the Tung-
hua Palace, and Director of Destinies*
by Anonymous (12th century)

The Book of Azure Emptiness
by Ch'en Nan (d. 1213)

The Book of Efficacious Seals for Penetrating Mystery
by Anonymous (date unknown)
>Includes instructions for turning red beans into soldiers by rubbing them with a specific mixture of sheep's blood, cow's bile, and mud, and pronouncing a formula over them.

The Book of the Dark Maiden
by Anonymous (4th century)
>Instructions for predicting ill-fated marriages.

The Book of the Six Yin of the Sublime Grotto, the True Scripture of the Hidden Days
by Anonymous (date unknown)
>Banned by the Department of Forbidden Books in 971.

The Cloud Bookcase with Seven Labels
edited by Chang Chün-fang (fl. 1008–1025)
>An anthology. A later commentator notes that several sections are divided into two parts ("Upper" and "Lower") for no apparent reason.

The Code of Nu-ch'ing for Controlling Demons
by Anonymous (3rd century)
>Lists 36,000 demons who can be warded off by knowing their names. The meaning of the word or name "Nu-ch'ing" is unknown.

Comprehensive Collection of True Facts Concerning the Land of Bliss
by Liu Tao-ming (c. 1291)

Diagrams Illustrating the Mystery of the Cultivation of Truth, the Mystery of the Supreme Pole, and the Mystery of the Primordial Chaos
by Anonymous (12th century)
  Contains only the diagrams with no explanations.

Dividing the Pear in a Period of Ten Days
by Wang Che (c. 1183)
  Collection of poems. The title refers to a pear that the author cut into fifty-five pieces to give to a disciple. On receiving the fifty-fifth piece, the disciple and his wife separated.

Essay on the Depths of the Mind in the Great Void
by Anonymous (date unknown)
  A series of twenty-word poems.

The Essence of the Supreme Secrets
by Anonymous (6th century)
  One-third of the original text is apparently missing.

Essentials for Preserving Life
by P'u Ch'ian-kuan (fl. 934–965)
  Recommends that "one should avoid noxious winds in the same way as one would avoid an arrow." Fruits, meat, fish and fowl may be eaten, but no vegetables.

Final Chapter of the Continued Explanations of the True Origin, the Great Cave, and the Highest Direction
by Anonymous (14th century)
  It is noted that there are no previous chapters to which this text corresponds.

Five Charms of the Mysterious Book
by Anonymous (4th century)
> The text includes only one charm.

The Forest of Changes
by Ch'iao Kan (1st century)

The Forest of Opinions
by Ma Yung (c. 787)

Gradual Enlightenment
by Ma Tan-yang (1123–1184)
> Contains poems where the first character is deliberately omitted.

Great Method of the Jade Hall of the Three Heavens of the Supreme Mysterious Origin
by Lu Shih-chung (c. 1158)
> Portions of the text were dictated to Lu by the Heavenly Lord Great
> Master of the Teaching, whose voice, to everyone else, sounded
> like a baby crying.

Handbook for Making Black Frost
by Anonymous (8th century)

Hymns to the Five Planets
attributed to Chang Heng (78–139)
> The text contains no hymns or poems to the planets. The attribu-
> tion to Chang Heng is undoubtedly false.

The Identity of Both
by Lo Yin (833–910)
> Often confused with *The Identity of Both* by Wu Yün (d. 778).

Illustrated Version of the Flight to the Sun and the Moon
by Anonymous (13th century)
  Describes a method for flying to the sun and the moon.

Instructions on the Emanations from the Labyrinth
by Anonymous (8th century)

The Marvelous Forest of the Great Vehicle
by Anonymous (8th century)
  Explains that the forest is located near the Palace of Primordial
  Yang in the City of the Seven Treasures on the Mountain of Unimaginable Discourse.

Marvelous Stanzas for Resuscitating Corpses
by Anonymous (8th century)
  A poem in twenty-eight stanzas.

Memorials that Proclaim Mercy and Are Helpful in Working Wonders
by Tu Kuang-t'ing (850–933)
  Includes a "Memorial to Arrest the Puppy Devil from Under the
  Stone" (a demon who attacks children). Demons responsible for
  children's diseases are also named, including the Wet Nurse from
  Heaven's Prison and the Washing Bride.

Mr. Chou's Records of His Communications with the Invisible World
by Chou Tzu-liang (497–516), edited and annotated by T'ao Hong-
ching (c. 517)
  The text was found in a mountain cave, after the author's suicide at
  age 19. The editor includes the formula for the poison the author
  took.

Notes to Be Kept Inside a Pillow
by Anonymous (9th century)

Penal Code of the Mysterious Capital
by Anonymous (7th century)

Poems Made While Beating the Ground
by Shao Yung, "Yao Fu" (1012–1077)
    A collection of some 1500 poems, including a series of 135 poems
    titled "Chants of Head and Tail," each one of which begins and
    ends with the line: "Yao Fu does not write poems merely for fun."

Questions of Mystery at Times of Serenity
by Po Yu-ch'an (fl. 1194–1229)

Register of Flying Steps of the Six Stars that Govern Fate
by Anonymous (date unknown)
    Instructions on meditating on the six stars of the fictitious South-
    ern Dipper. The stars should also be drawn on the soles of the feet.

Requisite Knowledge for the Alchemical Laboratory
by Wu Wu (c. 1163)
    Recommends that clean clothes always be worn in the laboratory,
    and no women, Buddhist monks, chickens, or dogs allowed to enter.

Rhapsody of the Gate of the Dark Female
by Yu Yen (fl. 1253–1296)

Rules on Purple Tablets: The Book of Blazing Light Created by Transformation
by Anonymous (4th century)
    The text purportedly materialized from a condensation of light
    and divine breath. Includes instructions on developing long-
    distance vision.

Scripture and Chart for the Contemplation of Man-Bird Mountain
by Anonymous (date unknown)

Scripture for Saving Deceased Parents from Distress in Future Lives
by Anonymous (8th century)

The Scripture of the Essentials of the Clear Mirror
by Anonymous (8th century)
   Instructions for seven methods for achieving immortality, presented in seven short paragraphs.

Scripture on the Recompense for Parental Kindness
by Chao I-chen (d. 1382)
   Recommends that pious sons and daughters perform a three-year fast, corresponding to the period when infants nurse. Author of *Returning to the Void*, fourteen poems of twenty-eight words each.

Secret Register for Obtaining Release from Incantations and Spells from All Quarters
by Anonymous (15th century)
   Advice for when one is "possessed by the spirits of earth altars, sacred areas, forest, brooks, wells, or stoves" or one is the victim of spells cast by the "devious masters of the vulgar cults of the River God."

Sesame Song
by Liu Ch'ung-yung (c. 931)
   Contains only one poem. Sesame is not mentioned.

Seven Recitations of the Divine Realm with 7 Transformations for Dancing in Heaven
by Anonymous (4th century)
   The latter section includes the method for transforming oneself into a cloud.

Song for Dispelling Doubts Concerning the Correct Path
by Chung-li Ch'üan (11th century)

A single poem, which commentators note completely contradicts ideas presented by the author in other poems.

Stabilizing the Creative Forces and Making the Numinous Powers Shine Brightly
by Anonymous (12th century)

Instructions for summoning the spirits of the stars of the Big Dipper.

Superior Book of the Flying Immortals by the Sovereign of Precious Truth Cinnabar Origin
by Anonymous (date unknown)

Exercises for the absorption of stellar effluvia.

Superior Scripture on the Dongfang Palace of the Brain
by Anonymous (4th century)

The title bears no relationship to the text.

Supplementary Book of the Master of the Obscure Truth
by Chang Chih-ho (fl. 752–762)

Contains three sections ("Blue Void," "Celestial Bird", and "Spirit of the Waves"). Uncertain to what it is a supplement.

Three Rhapsodies on the Origin of Chaos
by Shih Te-i (fl. 860–874)

The author found the book floating in a river, but it was not wet. That evening, the guardian of the book appeared to inform Shih that previous editions contained many mistakes and that this was the correct version.

Ten Charts for Perusal While Reclining
by Li Ssu-ts'ung (c. 1050)
  Author of *The Anthology of the Abyssal Cavern.*

Ten Rules for the Initial Stage of Perfection
by Anonymous (8th century)
  Other versions of this text contain eighty-one rules.

Treatise on the Art of Sitting and Forgetting
by Ssu-ma Ch'eng-chen (647–735)

Treatise on the Calculation of the Bushel in Purple Sublimity
by Anonymous (date unknown)
  Divination based on the layout of eighteen partially imaginary
  stars. The constellation the Bushel is not mentioned.

Treatise on the Planet Venus
by Anonymous (date unknown)
  Contains a list of ten types of people who will be either able or
  unable to understand the text.

*The True Method of Returning by Chariot and Completing the Way Accord-
ing to the Department of the Celestial Pivot*
by Anonymous (12th century)
  Contains a cure for insanity through handwriting analysis.

The True Scripture of the Great Cavern
by Anonymous (date unknown)
  Contains the Secret Formula of the Whirlwind.

The True Scripture of the White Monkey
by Anonymous (date unknown)
  A scripture revealed by a white monkey.

Glossary

Abanasong. The price to be paid when a man marries his deceased brother's widow.

Achhisa. Oath; curse.

Adeuna. An additional due payable when a woman marries into a strange village.

Ahrnaw. A vampire ghost.

Aitla. A platform outside a house.

Alangasi. An earthquake.

Amakia. A marriage procession.

Ana. Forbidden.

Anahmang. Forbidden things; the sacred vessels used for the Kli-azangpina sacrifice.

Angiapatli. Eavesdropping.

Angkia. Lit. "house enter." The most important part of a marriage price.

Angtong. House posts.

Angveu. Bamboos run over the rafters the length of a house.

Aoh. Rest; a holiday in consequence of a sacrifice; remaining within the house.

Aparupa. Theft.

Aphei. Adultery.

Arakhei. Elopement.

Asia. Oath; curse.

Asu. House post supporting the ridgepole.

Athikhi. Lit. "village of the dead." The afterworld.

Atu. A hoe.

Awhbeu. A hen basket.

Awrua. A pig killed by a man who has to pay certain marriage prices and the death due, and given by him to the man to whom he has to pay the price.

Awrudbawna. A small price which has to be paid by a person from whom a price is due to the recipient of the price. Until this price is paid the recipient refuses to eat the *awrua* pig.

Awsithleupa. A comet.

Bai. The basket used for measuring paddy, short for *tlabai*.

Barongthu. Botten pulse.

Batla. Beam of loom.

Beibei. Lit. "chief chief." The name of one part of the series of Kliangchei feasts.

Beiphia. A potter's mallet.

Beu. A mole on the face.

Biatai. A promise; an agreement to copulate; an agreement to pay.

Bongchhi. The sacred tree at the foot of which the Tleulia sacrifice is performed.

Bupa. The beer provided for a funeral feast.

Chahri. Rafters supporting the floor.

Chaka. Famine.

Chakei. A threshold; a tiger.

Ohakhaw. A shuttle.

Chanong chaichhi. A dowry.

Chawmman. Board and lodging charge.

Cheisia. A pellet bow.

Cheusapathaipa. Lit. "the pure man." The man who assists at a chief's Khazangpina.

Chiha. A fish weir.

Chheutheu. The day after Khisongbo and Tleulia when all the villagers go out to hunt.

Chheutlia. The red plume worn by a man who has taken a head.

Chhihrang. Green beads.

Chhongchhireu. Lit. "clan leave instead of." The death due payable on unmarried persons.

Chhongki. The name given to a man who has shot a prescribed number of wild animals and has thereby qualified to enter Paradise.

Chiami. A bugle.

Chilong. Flint.

Chipaleipa. An imbecile, a village idiot.

Chongtlapa. The man who kills, cuts up, and cooks pigs used for a feast.

Hawleupaka. The dead men's gate. The path taken by the spirits of the dead to Atikhi.

Hawmikah. A sacrifice to stop excessive rain.

Hladeu. Songs sung by successful warriors who have taken heads and by hunters who have bagged big game.

Hleiri. A cane suspension bridge.

Hmiachipaipa. The people with tattooed faces. Probably the Khyengs.

Hmiatla. Lit. "face happy." Compensation; peace offering; atonement price. A small amount payable for minor offences.

Hneuthli. An archer's bracer.

Hrahrachahno. Rape.

Hraisong. The post to which a mithun is tied up for sacrifice.

Hrangzonghna. Lit. "long life plant." A plant the root of which is eaten by women to enable them to rear their children.

Hrapaki. A man who has earned a place in paradise by killing certain animals. See *chhongki.*

Hri. An evil spirit which causes disease; the ability to cause a disease.

Hrilh. Period during which no work may be done.

Hrokei. A woman's hairpin.

Kadua. A friend.

Kahmi. A ladder.

Kalasapa. Lit. "long-haired foreigners." The Hughs.

Karo. A woman's pipe.

Karolusong. Small stick on which pipe bowls are shaped.

Kei. A friend.

Khabeirai. A brass beer pot.

Khapia. Cross beams supporting the floor of a house.

Khazanghneipa. A person who cures disease by divination.

Khazanghra. Lit. "God's darkness." The legendary darkness which fell upon the world.

Khazangpa. God.

Khazangpina. The sacrifice to God.

Kheitiri. A yellow bead.

Khisong. Lit. "village magnificent." An important spirit and its abode. (Mountain peaks, caves, precipices, deep pools in rivers are *khisong*.)

Khitiawnah. Lit. "rain calling." Sacrifices for rain.

Khuthang. A puggree.

Khiithi. Impotence.

Kiali. A brass basin.

Kihlong. A conch shell.

Kihlong. A thread winder.

Kohrei. A woman's coat.

Kumasaparu. Theft of an animal from another's trap.

Laba. A thread holder.

Ladaw. A pair of brass gongs.

Lahmi. A spindle.

Laisa. A girl.

Laisacharei. Courting.

Laitleu. A spinster.

Lakah. The bow used for flicking cotton.

Lakhang. A girl's headdress worn at dances and weddings.

Lakhu. A rain hat.

Lasawng. A spindle and thread.

Lavaong. A quiver.

Lawbu. Bar of loom.

Lawhna. Heddle.

Leichkang. A case before the chief.

Leu. A fine inflicted on any one refusing to do village work.

Leuchapa. An envoy. A go-between.

Leurahripa. A spirit of the mountains, woods or streams.

Lianeu. Murder.

Liari. The umbilical cord.

Litang. Lit. "bow swing." A method of finding out what sacrifice to perform to cure a sick man.

Litangthaipa. A man who is able to ascertain the right sacrifice to perform to cure a sick man.

Longbeu. Edible clay.

Longpa. A stone trap.

Longrai. A beer pot.

Longtang. A marriage memorial.

Luteu. The compensation payable to the relations of a murdered man.

Maichhangna. Lit. "name remembrance." The death price due on unmarried persons.

Maluaong. A woman who has survived two or three husbands.

Matlei. Lit. "price divided." The term applied when a man divides up his daughter's price with his sons or brothers.

Nangcheu. The portion of a marriage price taken by the bride's paternal aunt.

Nangchhikhawpa. Lit. "sun door shutter." The black dwarfs who open and close the doorway of the sun.

Nanghlo. A present payable to the persons accompanying a man collecting a debt in another village.

Nangti. A little demon who lives in a hollow tree stump full of water.

Narongsakeu. Lit. "sister wild animal loin." The meat due payable by a man to his wife's sister; it consists of the tail and the meat around its base.

Nawdong. Lit. "baby soft." A child that dies within two or three days of birth.

Nawkhutlong. The ten days after childbirth, during which neither the mother nor the child may leave the house.

Ngazuasaphei. Lit. "niece's hind leg." The meat due payable to a man's sisters and sister's daughters.

Ngiapareu. Adultery.

Nongcheu. The portion of a marriage price taken by the bride's mother or by the bride's mother's sister.

Nonghia. Marriage.

Nonghmei. Widow.

Nonghrang. Wife.

Nongthang. Concubine.

Palaphei. The weft.

Palatong. The warp.

Puna. Sacred; holy; taboo; the condition of a man who has just performed or is performing a sacrifice.

Panglukhu. Cloth to cover the head, payable to a cuckold by the man who has slept with the wife.

Parunawtapa. Lit. "a little theft." Breaking wind.

Pathlong. Ridge pole.

Patho. Reed for sucking up rice beer.

Peira. Paradise.

Peuchi. Dark blue thread.

Phavaw. The parts of a sacrifice set aside for the god.

Phiatla. A gourd spoon.

Phipahripa. Flying white ants.

Photkt. Cymbals.

Puma. The maternal uncle's portion of a marriage price.

Pumtek. A much valued black-and-white bead.

Rabong. Plume of scarlet horse tail worn by a man who has taken a head.

Racha. Beer pot.

Raha. Spinning wheel.

Rahathua. Spindle.

Rahong. Brass basin.

Raitapa. Small beer pot.

Reipaso. Courting, seduction.

Riasaw. Lit. "scabies son." A bastard.

Riathama. Lit. "scabies price." The bastard's price.

Riha. Lit. "corpse for." The animal killed to accompany a dead person to the abode of the dead.

Rithu. A chaperone. The man who has to look after the young girls attending a wedding to see that they behave.

Sabai. Rice due payable to a chief.

Sachakeu. The method of harvesting by knocking off the grain with a stick into the basket.

Sahaw. The meat due payable to a chief on all wild animals killed by his subjects.

Sahma. Rice beer.

Sahmaphopa. The man who carries the beer pot in a wedding procession.

Sahrualua. A winnowing platform.

Sahu. The breath of a large animal.

Sakia. Man's brass hairpin.

Sapahktisapa. The person who performs a sacrifice to call the spirits of wild animals.

Sapalong. The chest of a wild animal, always given to the shooter's maternal uncle.

Sarang. The last time a boy's hair is cut before it is tied up in a topknot.

Saw. A dangerous property attaching to the ghosts of people dying unnatural deaths, whether in war or by accident, and also to certain living persons, such as captives.

Sawkahrong. Bamboo or wooden hairpin.

Sawvaw. An unnatural death.

Sepi. A mithun cow.

Seu. A sharpened bamboo stake used as a defense in war.

Sikhai. A wooden wedge used for splitting tree trunks.

Sisakuchakhi. A pumtek bead bracelet payable to a cuckold by the man who has seduced his wife.

Sochiphang. A netting spool.

Songkho. Paddy mortar.

Sokaw. A fishing net.

Sopi. A large fishing net.

Takangpa. The Chakmas. (The first Chakma seen was standing on the bank of a river breaking water snail's shells, and the name is derived from the noise made by the shells breaking.)

Tangta. A one-stringed violin.

Tatangteuleupa. Lit." the ghost's earrings." Artificial flowers made out of bamboo and many colored threads, used when dancing the Rakhatla dance at a funeral.

Thai. Loom.

Thaipho. Leather belt worn by women weaving.

Thaipahniapa. Sharp-edged split bamboo used for shaping pipe bowls.

Thaisapa. Weaver.

Thapachhi. Defamation.

Theipipakia. A poisoned arrow.

Thlachhi. A mischievous soul.

Thlapha. A good soul.

Thlathleu. Lit. "soul hold." A sacrifice performed to prevent a man's soul from wandering, generally performed for persons who have been in trouble.

Thuasang. A dao sent to a woman's parents by her suitor when proposing marriage.

Thupahama. Lit. "smell breathe price." The reward payable to a woman who opens a burial vault and makes it ready for the next occupant.

Tieipaei. Ordeal by boiling water.

Tikupa. Lit. "the men with large testicles." The Tipperahs.

Tilaipi. The sea.

Tini. The paternal aunt's portion of a marriage price.

Tipang. A lake.

Tipani. Lit. "water to drink." The ceremony of giving rice beer to the bride and bridegroom at a wedding.

Tlaikopa. Lit. "the naked men." The Lusheis.

Tlaraihria. Village work.

Tlaraipasi. Village sacrifice to prevent epidemics.

Tleuhmia. The ground directly in front of a house.

Tleulia. The open place in the center of a village where sacrifices are performed.

Tlongang. Lit. "reach house." Hospitality.

Tongkdhngpa. Thunder.

Acknowledgments

Some of these essays first appeared in *5 Plus* (Germany), *Artes de México*, *Conjunctions, Edit* (Germany), *Harper's, Higher Arc* (Australia), *Lettera Internazionale* (Italy), *Lettre International* (Germany), *Little Star, The London Review of Books, El Malpensante* (Colombia), *Le Monde Diplomatique* (Germany), *The New York Review of Books*, and *Síbila* (Spain); online in *Alligatorzine* (Belgium), *Asian Cha, China File*, the *Harper's* blog, the *LRB* blog, and *Napalm Health Spa*; and in my books *Orangen! Erdnüsse!*, translated by Peter Torberg (Berenberg Verlag, Germany, 2011), *Wildlife* (Giramondo, Australia, 2012), *Las Cataratas*, translated by Aurelio Major (Ed. Duomo, Spain, 2012), *Two American Scenes* (with Lydia Davis, New Directions, 2013), *The Wall, the City, and the World* (Readux, Germany, 2014), and *Vogelgeister*, translated by Beatrice Fassbender (Verlag der Buchhandlung Klaus Bittner, Germany, 2014).

Some are adapted from introductions to Jeffrey Yang, *Ein Aquarium*, (Berenberg Verlag, Germany, 2012); Herbert Read, *The Green Child* (New Directions, 2013); Andrew Schelling, editor, *Love and the Turning Seasons* (Counterpoint, 2014); Charles Reznikoff, *Testimony* (Black Sparrow/David Godine, 2015); and Víctor Terán and David Shook, editors, *Like A New Sun: New Mexican Indigenous Poetry* (Phoneme, 2015).

"The Ghosts of Birds" was written for the catalog of an exhibition by the Maori painter Shane Cotton, *The Hanging Sky*, at the Christchurch Gallery, New Zealand, 2013, and refers to some of the images in his paintings. "A Calendar of Stones" was written for the catalog of an exhibition by Teresita Fernández, *As Above, So Below*, at the Massachusetts Museum of Contemporary Art, 2014. "The Wall" is adapted from the exhibition *Aus anderer Sicht: Die frühe Berliner Maurer/ The Other View: The Early Berlin Wall*, conceived and curated by Annett Gröschner and Arwed Messmer, and the 750-page catalog of documentation, published by Hatje Cantz in 2011. "The City" was written for the Souk Ukaz, "Writing In and Beyond the City," in Fez, Morocco, in 2009. "Islands in the Sea" was written for the first issue of *Stonecutter*, 2011, edited by Katie Raissian.

The first section is a continuation of the serial essay *An Elemental Thing*.